Knead to Know...more

Your microbakery handbook

Chris Young and bakers of the Real Bread Campaign

What bakers said about the original Knead to Know

> "The most practical book for anyone thinking of starting a bakery enterprise."

Emma Parkin,
Emma's Bread, Exeter

> "There are lots of books with bread recipes in them, but only one with a bakehouse recipe."

Alex Lister,
Rise Artisan Bakehouse,
Durham

> "The book was invaluable to me when I was starting Wild Bread."

James Thorn,
Wild Bread, Faversham

> "Knead to Know was massively helpful when I started the Stoneham Bakehouse journey."

Simon Cobb,
Stoneham Bakehouse, Hove

> "This book was a gold mine for us, back in the day."

Max Tobias,
The Dusty Knuckle, London

> "The book was biblical for my personal journey!"

Jo Bottrill,
Jo's Loaves, Bedfordshire

Contents

Intro

Foreword

This is a remarkable book. Not only because knowhow springs from every page and transforms into practical wisdom before our eyes, but because it has been fermented by the desire to do good. There's plenty about the practicalities of running a small baking business, of course. There is also realism about the need to make a fair return, whatever the scale. But what makes this a vital manual for our troubled times is its spirit of companionship and mutual aid – celebrating and supporting the collective endeavour to nourish ourselves and our fellow citizens with Real Bread.

"This is not a baking book!", we are told on the back cover. Nor is it about 'start-up' businesses. This is, rather, a book for and by *upstarts* – people who determine to bake and share good bread and, sometimes to their own surprise, find themselves becoming part of a little, local, benign revolution. For one thing is clear: fighting corporate monocultures won't feed people better or more fairly; replacing them is the only way.

Becoming part of a new ecology of better grain and bread is hard work. The transformation of simple ingredients into something life-giving involves many agents working together. So it is encouraging that the collective experience and advice of the many micro, artisan and community bakers quoted in this greatly expanded edition of Knead to Know adds up to a resounding confirmation that it is *worth it*: this work, this bread, changes lives.

Ten years ago, we were just beginning to understand the importance of bacterial diversity in soils, cereals, sourdoughs and stomachs. The role of well-fermented food in supporting good gut-brain signalling confirms the 'therapeutic' value, explained in these pages as being as much to do with the baker as the baked-for, of making Real Bread with and for others.

Grasp this volume with your hands – it is a manual, after all – and you will learn as much about the *why* as the *how*.

Andrew Whitley *is the co-founder of Bread Matters, the Real Bread Campaign and Scotland the Bread.*

Introduction

The Real Bread Campaign's overarching mission is to find and share ways to make bread better for us, better for our communities and better for the planet. We define Real Bread as made without so-called processing aids or other additives, and work towards everyone having the chance to choose it. An element of this is informing, inspiring and promoting the microbakers who are instrumental in putting Real Bread back at the hearts of local communities around the UK and beyond.

Who is this for?

Got the hang of crafting consistently great Real Bread, feel you're now ready to start selling it, but are hesitant about getting the lease on that boarded-up shop on the high street? Maybe your microbakery business is up and running already and you're thinking of expanding and taking on employees. This book's not just for Real Bread bakers, either. Much of it is relevant whatever type of baking you do or type of small food business yours is, so step this way...

What is a microbakery?

That depends on who you're asking. When people in our circles talk about a microbaker, they're usually referring to a sole trader making up to a few dozen loaves in their home kitchen oven each weekend, or as often as the local farmers' market runs. There are variations, such as roping in a family member, friend or three; using a garage, shed or even small commercial space; getting a 'semi-pro' oven; baking hundreds of loaves; and perhaps operating on a full-time basis. For more see page 50.

Flip, dip and skip

I've laid out the business sections roughly in the order that a microbaker might need to know things. The first section is mainly geared to the sole trader running a microbakery from home, but also looks at other types of bakeries and business models run in different locations and by more people. The second bit is about scaling up. There is, however, stuff in all three sections that should be of use, or at

...east interest, wherever you are on your bakery business journey, which might well not follow the same order or path. Please do dip in and out, flip back and forth and skip bits altogether as suits you.

Is this everything I need to know?

Nope. Rather than aiming to be a fully comprehensive manual for starting and running your own business, this is an introductory guide. It is a buffet of tasters with pointers to where you can find out more about the topics you find the most appetising. I'll *try* to rein in the puns, metaphors and other wordplay from here on in...

While I've included a few loaf recipes, this isn't a baking book – there are plenty out there already, including our own (plug, plug) Slow Dough: Real Bread. Importantly, reading is no substitute for rolling up your sleeves and getting stuck in. You'll learn some of the most important lessons in your own bakehouse. Bakers have told us that they have also found it extremely useful to spend time alongside experienced bakers, either on a course or working (or volunteering) in a bakery.

When should I quit my day job?

How long is a ficelle? There's no 'normal' or 'typical' to this: when, where and how your bakery business develops is up to you. You're in charge of the pace, scale and direction of development. You might race from hobby baker, via home-based microbaker, to owning a bakery on the high street in 12 months, or it could take years until you move (or get kicked) out of your kitchen. The again, you might keep clocking in at the office, with your bakery staying as a weekend side hustle. If you do plan to quit the day job and rely instead on your microbakery income, though, please be sure to do your sums as part of your business planning – see page 43.

Reality check

While we don't want to discourage anyone, we also want to be sure that people are realistic. Turning a baking hobby into a financially sustainable business is hard. It requires a considerable investment of your time, money and self. This is true for the home-based weekend microbaker and even more so if and when you scale things up.

Beyond Blighty

Though the Real Bread Campaign has a network of supporters around the world, the majority are in Britain. I have, however, expanded the scope of this revised edition to include crumbs of information applicable to some of the other countries where we have supporters and the original edition of this book sold well: Australia, Canada, Ireland, New Zealand and the USA. Wherever on our small planet you are, I hope that you'll find plenty here to help supplement and stimulate your own research.

If you have any information, insight and advice from your own experience that you would be happy for us to help you share, or if you have feedback about this book, please email realbread@sustainweb.org

Happy baking!

Chris Young, Penge, October 2021

Join us

Everyone is invited to join the Real Bread Campaign as a supporter, whether on behalf of a bakery, mill, other business or organisation, or simply because they believe in the Campaign's work. Campaign supporters receive our quarterly magazine, *True Loaf*, and have access to The Real Baker-e online forum, where they can ask for, and share, knowledge and advice with fellow supporters. It's also where we post information that we believe might be of use, or at least interest, to people involved in the rise of Real Bread. As a thank you, we work to secure supporter discounts on ingredients, equipment, classes and more. Alternatively, you can sign up as a Campaign friend to receive *Breadcrumbs*, our free e-newsletter.

Since our launch in November 2008, we've welcomed thousands of paying supporters from more than 20 countries, and friends in many more. At the time of writing, we are looking at how we can inspire and support people to start their own national or regional Real Bread networks outside the UK. To learn all about the Campaign, our work, our latest news and how to join us, please visit www.realbreadcampaign.org

We'd also love you to stay connected with us, #RealBreadCampaign supporters and the wider #RealBread movement through social media:

Facebook & Instagram @RealBreadCampaign   Twitter @RealBread

Get Real!

As everyone has their own idea of what Real Bread is and what the Campaign stands for, we wanted to put it down on paper so that we're all on the same page.

What is Real Bread?

The Campaign simply defines Real Bread as made without any so-called 'processing aid' or other additive.

In fact, we believe that 'no additives' should be a key criterion in the legal definition of bread, full stop. Why should bakers who lovingly craft bread in a time-honoured, natural way have to qualify it with 'real', 'artisan', 'craft' and the like? We say: reclaim the noble name 'bread' and leave it to the industrial loaf fabricators to come up with a new name for their additive-laden products.

At its most basic, bread can be crafted from just flour and water, from which an unleavened flatbread can be made, or a sourdough starter culture nurtured. In practice, the addition of a little salt is something that very few bakers (or bread lovers) would do without. Chemical raising agents (eg baking powder/soda) aren't used in Real Bread making, but bakers may use commercial yeast instead of a sourdough starter to leaven some, or all, of their dough. They might also choose to add seeds, nuts, herbs, oils, fruit, vegetables, eggs, dairy products or other natural ingredients.

Bread is almost universal across nations, cultures, ethnic groups, genders, belief systems and income levels. Our inclusive definition reflects this: it doesn't necessarily have to be basket-proved, stoneground, wholemeal, heritage wheat sourdough, handmade by an artisan and baked in a wood-fired oven! As long as it's made without additives, it's what we call bread, be that a bagel, lavash, crumpet, focaccia, roti, matzo, injera, tortilla, naan, bao, kisra, shokupan, white sandwich tin loaf... the list goes on and on around the globe.

I wanna bake (g)free

Contrary to some people's belief, there is such a thing as gluten-free Real Bread. Sadly, people who have to avoid gluten find it even harder to get Real Bread than the rest of us. The g-free market is also dominated by industrial loaf fabricators and millers, who tend to use highly-refined starches propped up by additives - xanthan gum, hydroxypropyl methyl cellulose, glycerol and so on.

We're not denying that there are extra challenges to making Real Bread without gluten (especially if trying to replicate a wheat-based, white sandwich loaf) but it can be - and is - done. There are naturally gluten-free flours out there and, though we've only come across a handful of bakers making gluten-free Real Bread, in some parts of the world it's a staple - take injera, for example. For more information about making delicious, nutritious gluten-free Real Bread look up Naomi Devlin in the UK and Chris Stafferton in Tasmania.

The Chorleywood 'Bread' Process

This was devised in the late 1950s by the British Baking Industries Research Association, then based in the Hertfordshire town from which the process takes its name, and unleashed in July 1961. CBP replaces natural dough development and fermentation time with high-speed mixing and higher levels of yeast than Real Bread making, to inflate the dough quickly.

The dough for this ultra-processed food product is usually laced with any number of additives from the industry's arsenal, some of which UK law allows manufacturers to leave off the label. They help the dough withstand the stresses of the process, making it stretchy to rise high and quickly, then tighten up to stay risen, and help the finished loaf to stay softer longer, yet with the strength to withstand a cold, hard buttering. Softer, stronger, longer. Is it just us, or does that sound like a toilet paper advert?

The loaf fabrication industry defends its use of additives, laughably comparing them to baking powder used by cake makers at home. The oft trotted out 'only used in small quantities to help the natural process' defence isn't one that would work for dope cheat athletes and doesn't wash with us, either. What are the long-term effects of constant consumption of such a cocktail? Could the virtual elimination of fermentation, or the additives themselves, account for the difficulty in stomaching industrial loaf products that some people report? See the next chapter for more on this. If calcium propionate and so on are indispensable saviours preventing food waste, why is it that the factory loaf is one of the most wasted food products in the UK?

The state of our loaf life

Long gone are the days when every loaf eaten in the UK came fresh from the local bakery or home oven, made with nothing but natural ingredients, time and care. If you believe figures touted by the baking industry, today around 80% of loaf production is controlled by a handful of industrial loaf fabricators. Collectively they churn out perhaps 12 million wrapped, sliced, additive-laden Chorleywood Process (see panel) loaves each day from remote, highly-automated factories.

Supermarket in-store bakeries might account for a further 15-17% of production. Even many of these loaves are manufactured using additives in out-of-town factories. Chilled or frozen products are transported around the country (or even internationally) to be baked again in-store using what we call 'loaf tanning salons'. Such products are often marketed using claims such as 'freshly baked' and 'artisan', competing directly with genuine artisan bakers who truly do make bread fresh from scratch. You can find reports from our investigations into such practices on our website. The picture is apparently similar in a growing number of other countries.

This leaves perhaps 3-5% of the pie for SME bakeries, though in over a decade we've not found a single Real Bread bakery whose sales figures have been taken into account by any market researcher. Nobody (including the Office of National Statistics) even seems to have an accurate figure for the number of SME bakery businesses in the UK. It's clear from conversations we've had with the Craft Bakers Association that many of their members don't make what we call Real Bread – see page 131.

A desire to enjoy all–natural food

Countless generations eating Real Bread have proved beyond any doubt that, for the vast majority of people, it's delicious and nutritious.

By contrast, an additive only undergoes a relatively short period of testing before being declared safe (or, in the more pragmatic terminology of the US Food and Drink Administration, "generally recognised as safe") before being unleashed on the market. What's not been tested in any controlled way is the effect on the human body of the cocktail of additives used in ultra-processed industrial foods. A 2018 study of 44,551 French adults concluded, however, that a 10% increase in the consumption of ultra-processed food was associated with a 14% higher risk of mortality.

What's declared safe today might not be considered so tomorrow. History is littered with non-food substances used in industrial food processing that manufacturers defended but were then forced to withdraw due to public pressure or a change in law. Think of azodicarbonamide, benzoyl peroxide, Agene (nitrogen trichloride) and chlorine-based bleaching agents for bread flour. All were once declared safe by scientists and industrial loaf fabricators, but then dropped or banned in the UK and some other countries due to evidence of possible negative effects on human health, ranging from impaired endocrine function to neurological disease. The International Agency for Research on Cancer even listed one flour additive, potassium bromate, as possibly carcinogenic to humans.

Understanding that shoppers can find lists of unfamiliar names or E-numbers off-putting, manufacturers now often turn to what are termed 'processing aids'. In food law, this is a category of additives (often added enzymes) that do not need to be included on an ingredients list. Suppliers often market these as 'clean label' or 'label friendly'. You can read more about the questions hanging over processing aids and other additives on the Marketing and Labelling pages in the About section of our website.

Quality and taste

Quality and taste are both subjective; everyone has a personal set of - often subconscious - criteria for each. It's probable that an industrial loaf company will defend the quality of its loaves on the grounds of being produced uniformly and hygienically. Likewise, someone who has only ever eaten - or has lingering fond childhood associations with - Chorleywood Process loaf products might find comfort and pleasure in their familiar texture and taste... or perhaps lack thereof.

It's not just factory loaf buyers and manufacturers who think like this. Unlike many of their continental counterparts, some bakers of the 20th century British 'craft' tradition still find it hard to shake off the received 'wisdom' that an off-white crumb with large, irregular holes and a tangy taste are 'faults'. Then again, some of their number are now throwing in concentrates or packet mixes, advertised to them as providing shortcuts to making 'artisan sourdough' and the like. No need to gain the extra bread making skills and knowledge developed over time by a true artisan baker, they are told, despite an artisan baker being the key ingredient in genuine artisan bread. We invite them to kick the additive habit to get real!

As a Real Bread baker, your best bet for satisfying yourself that you are baking the tastiest, best quality loaves that you can is to listen to other Real Bread bakers, your customers and your own instinct. Entering your bread in reputable food or baking awards can be a way of getting useful feedback too.

The Real Bread Campaign

The Real Bread Campaign was co-founded in November 2008 by Real Bread baker, teacher and advocate, Andrew Whitley and Sustain: the alliance for better food and farming, the UK-based charity that runs the Campaign.

Our mission is to find and share ways to make bread better for us, better for our communities and better for the planet.

Our initiatives include:

#RealBreadWeek and **#SourdoughSeptember** Annual, international celebrations of additive-free loaves and the people who make them, encouraging people to buy Real Bread from local, independent bakeries, bake their own and pass on baking skills and knowledge.

Honest Crust Act Lobbying in the UK for improved loaf labelling and marketing legislation to protect people's right to make better informed choices about the loaves and sandwiches they buy, while also challenging manufacturers and retailers on misleading loaf marketing and incomplete/absent ingredient labelling.

Together We Rise Helping more people living with mental health issues, and a range of other challenges, benefit from the therapeutic, employment and social opportunities of making Real Bread.

No Loaf Lost Moving upstream from dealing with food waste to helping bakeries reduce the amount of surplus they produce in the first place.

Better Bred Bread What can be, and is being done, to improve the health and nutritional properties of bread? What research is needed to back up existing evidence around, for example, sourdough fermentation and heritage/non-commodity grains to form conclusive proof?

Bakery support Through all of the above, the Real Bread Map, Real Bread Loaf Mark scheme, The Real Baker-e forum, this book and more, we promote, unite and support the people behind the rise of Real Bread, and the small bakeries that help create more jobs per loaf and keep our high streets alive.

Better for us

> **"** Sometimes it feels almost like we're providing therapy in a warm paper bag."

Handmade Bakery co-founder Dan McTiernan

Beyond all-natural loaves, a Real Bread baker can choose to offer people some, or all, of the following benefits:

- Loaves made from flours with higher nutritional value and levels of dietary fibre than highly-refined, roller-milled, modern wheat flour.
- High quality, delicious bread that elevates eating above mere nutritional necessity to a pleasurable activity.
- Organic loaves, which will have supported nature-friendly production and have lower levels of (if any) potentially harmful agrochemical residues in the food itself.

Also see the notes on page 231 about the possible health and nutritional benefits of longer fermentation.

Better for our communities

Small, local, independent Real Bread bakeries support more jobs per loaf than industrial production. We would like to see more neighbourhood bakeries that will create and sustain more jobs in total.

Campaign co-founder Andrew Whitley estimates that, in the appropriate setting, a Real Bread baker can handcraft something like 200 loaves per day. Relocalisation of the UK's current national daily output of around 12 million (mostly industrial) loaves at the hands of such bakers could, therefore, support jobs for 60,000 of them. If we add an extra 25% to our Real Bread army to cover days off for holidays and sickness, the number goes up to 75,000. That's 142% more than the 31,000 people the Office of National Statistics stated were employed as "bakers and flour confectioners" (ie the entire baking industry, including cakers and biscuiteers) between April 2018 and March 2019.

In addition to this quantitative measure, we believe that the skills and knowledge accumulated and used by Real Bread bakers has enormous qualitative value; a stimulating and fulfilling occupation supports mental wellbeing. Surely building and using one's skills and knowledge to craft Real Bread is more fulfilling than, say, overseeing a fully automated, computer-controlled industrial loaf production line or loading ready-made products into a supermarket loaf tanning salon?

We also believe that a small bakery can be of greater benefit to the rest of the people in its local community as it can:

- Mean more money is spent and reinvested in the local economy.
- Be a hub that plays a role in community cohesion and creates opportunities for social interaction.
- Help to support other good food growers, producers and other suppliers.
- Offer a shorter commute for its workers and shorter shopping trip for customers (perhaps even a walk or cycle ride) than to a distant factory or supermarket, which could offer environmental and well-being benefits.

A number of Real Bread bakeries also have a track record of creating training and employment opportunities for people having a tougher time than most of us. The owner might even deem generating this social 'profit' to be as important as a financial one and run the business as a social enterprise – read more on page 51.

Better for the planet

The following are steps that we encourage *all* bakeries to consider taking:

- Selling at the heart of a residential area, making it easier for people to shop by foot or by bike.
- Eliminating plastic (and reducing other) packaging.
- Choosing reusable packaging (eg offering customers a bag for life/loaf) and/or recycled materials that are also fully biodegradable.
- Using organic ingredients that have a lower (or zero) input of petrochemical fertilisers, pesticides, fungicides and herbicides.
- Choosing heritage wheats and ancient grains, which are naturally predisposed to thriving in organic systems, typically have very good micronutrient profiles, and can be enjoyed by some people who struggle with modern wheat varieties.
- Sourcing flour from local mills, ideally produced from locally grown grain using truly renewable sources of energy – eg wind or water power.
- Working to reduce energy consumption at all stages of production – the Carbon Trust can help with this.
- Opting for greener sources for as much energy as possible, such as wood and biomass from sustainable sources or, better still, fully renewable sources – wind, water, solar, hydroelectric etc. Using biodiesel from recycled cooking

oil (not from crops that could have been used as food or from land that could have been used for food production or was once rainforest...) to power delivery vehicles.

Consider publishing, following and continually reviewing an environmental – or wider ethical – policy. Examples of bakeries doing this include Hobbs House Bakery, The Thoughtful Bakery and Martins Bakery.

The importance of time

By Real Bread Campaign co-founder Andrew Whitley.

Real Bread making is essentially the transformation of flour and water into a different, more edible, state by the application of various forms of energy over time. This transformation usually involves the biological process of fermentation, the by-products of which include the gas that aerates the structure of leavened bread.

Time is an essential component of this process. It allows yeasts (either present in the flour – nurtured as a sourdough starter culture – or added as baker's yeast) to produce carbon dioxide gas. In the case of sourdough bread, if given long enough, naturally occurring lactic acid bacteria affect proteins in the dough and contribute to the bread's flavour, texture, nutritional quality and perhaps digestibility.

Bread can be made in a great variety of styles and shapes, but the underlying objective – to render flour and water appetising by trapping gas in the structure and then baking a crust around it – is constant. The Real Bread baker's skill lies in working with the natural properties of simple foods (like wheat and rye) and allowing time for natural processes to deliver the best possible results.

By contrast, chemical and enzyme-based dough-modifiers (categorised as 'improvers', emulsifiers, flour treatment agents and so on) replace some of both the baker's skill and time by manipulating the physical and chemical structure of dough to a uniform specification, without the need for significant fermentation. Such additives are excluded from the Campaign's definition of Real Bread because:

- While they might serve technical purposes in the quest for profit maximisation, they are totally unnecessary – as above, all you need to make delicious, leavened bread is flour, water, salt, time and yeast in some form.
- They are either derived from substances that play no part in healthy human nutrition (ie they are not foodstuffs) and/or they are biochemically manipulated for functional effect, perhaps without a full investigation of any potentially negative effects on human digestion.
- Their use almost always circumvents the process of prolonged fermentation, which is required to deliver the optimum benefits of bread to the people who eat it.

Starting out

Home is where the start is

For any baker, the cost of buying or renting a space to do the doughy deed can be one of their biggest business overheads. For the budding newbie microbaker, the cost of commercial property is usually prohibitive, so some creative thinking is needed to find a suitable and financially viable space for your start-up. This might well be in your own home.

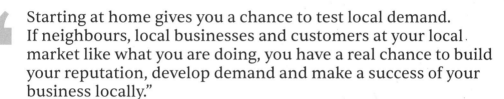

> Starting at home gives you a chance to test local demand. If neighbours, local businesses and customers at your local market like what you are doing, you have a real chance to build your reputation, develop demand and make a success of your business locally."

Jane Mason, Virtuous Bread

Your bakehouse

Call it a bakehouse or bakery, this is where the baking happens. Where you choose to make your bread depends on factors including the type and amount of baking you'll be doing and your business model.

When planning to start a microbakery from home, things to think about include:

- Clean and dry storage area(s) for ingredients and equipment, free from pests and pets. Ideally, your microbakery ingredients and kit should be separate from those you use domestically, though this might not be entirely possible – particularly when it comes to your oven.
- Refrigeration space, especially if you plan to retard dough (see pages 169 & 224).
- Recycling, composting and other waste disposal facilities. Your local authority might insist that you arrange (and perhaps pay for) them as a business user, rather than just chucking it all in with your domestic waste collection.
- Your electrical supply needs to be suitable for the type and amount of equipment you're using, with an appropriate number of power points in suitable locations, rather than umpteen plugs in adapters. You might find that a single-phase domestic supply is sufficient, but larger equipment, such as deck ovens and large mixers, are likely to draw more power and may require a three-phase supply. Ask an electrician or your equipment supplier to advise.

- • Water, drainage and sewerage appropriate to the size of your operation. You might be required to install a separate sink for handwashing. Your service provider might insist that you pay business, rather than domestic, rates.
- • National and local regulations around running a small business – health and safety etc. See the I fought the law section starting on page 101.
- • Tax and insurance implications.
- • Your neighbours, particularly if you're setting up a new business in a residenti area. Will the business mean you are creating extra noise (deliveries, customer coming and going etc), baking/cooking smells and so on?

Also try to think about, and plan well ahead for, how your business will grow. You want to put yourself in the best position to avoid equipping (and perhaps even renting or buying) a space that you outgrow before the oven's fully warmed up. Conversely, you don't want to create overheads or debts that your income won't cover soon enough.

*The words bakery and bakehouse both can be used for a retail space (eg shop, café or collection point) as well. As neither term has a legal definition in the UK, some retailers use them to refer to what we call loaf tanning salons, and even to places in which no baking is done at all.

Domestic kitchen

This is perhaps the most common place for microbakers to start experimenting. It's an excellent place for figuring out whether running a baking business is something you really want to – and can – do. Not only does it minimise your initial financial outlay, but the commute is also very short. The hours and money you would have spent travelling and renting space are yours to do with as you wish. Some microbakers find their home so suitable for their business that they never leave, though they may later buy a larger oven and extra equipment. Some take over another room in the house, or convert their garage or shed, to increase capacity and reduce domestic disruption.

A disadvantage might be the space available in a domestic oven and kitchen, limiting how much bread you can bake in one batch and how much room you have for equipment on your surfaces and in your cupboards. You also need to bear in mind how well your microbakery activities fit in with the rest of the household, particularly any early morning/late night baking you do, and around mealtimes. Work/life separation is another issue worth considering. Running a small business can become a 24/7 undertaking, so having the ability to physically close the door on your workspace and walk away can be beneficial.

" Starting small and building slowly allows you to get used to gradually increased volumes, especially if you have little or no experience in a commercial baking environment. There was no commute, which was good for me as I had a young family and could be there to help with parenting more than if I was working away from home. A downside of working from home is that it's difficult to turn off and leave work behind. I always found myself trying to get ahead by doing extra stuff, even if it didn't actually save me any time in the long run. Another disadvantage is that it's harder and harder to keep up with growing demand as there is only so much equipment you can fit into a home setting."

Adam Pagor, Grain and Hearth, Whitstable

" The domestic kitchen can be viewed as a good testing ground. Not only does it test resolve and commitment but, more importantly, it also shows the need for consistency. If you have been knocking out large amounts from inadequate facilities and managed some level of consistency, you are halfway there. In escalating the business by finding bigger premises and investing in a better oven and some real bakery machinery, you will easily achieve the consistency required."

Paul Merry, Panary, Dorset

" When I started out, the learning curve was extremely steep. Working from home I was lucky enough to have the support of my partner on the premises. The emotional support was hugely valuable."

Ian Waterland, Knead Good Bread, Leicestershire

Working in my home kitchen allowed me to conduct my consulting business from my home office. I found the hands-on bread work to be the perfect balance for the work at my computer."

Mark Stambler, Le Pagnol, California

Garage or other outbuilding

If you have access to one (and you can address any objections to you taking over some or all of it) a garage or outbuilding can be a good option. If you are granted sole use of the space, you won't need to pack your equipment away after each baking session. If your garage is large enough, it might even be possible to build a partition wall relatively easily and cheaply to section off a niche for your bakery.

Extra considerations related to this option might include:

- Heating it in winter and perhaps keeping it cool in summer.
- Having power, water and drainage installed.
- Security, particularly if you install expensive equipment.
- Whether you need planning permission or have to jump through any other regulatory loopholes.

You can read about other places for setting up, and expanding, your bakery in the section about scaling up, starting on page 156.

Equipment

When you think about it, all you really *need* to make bread are the means to measure, mix, prove, shape and then cook the ingredients. This could be as simple as hands, work surface and oven*.

What other bits of kit you might need or choose to acquire depends on factors such as the type of products you'll be making, how many you intend to produce at a time, the space you have to work in and what you want to acquire to make your job easier.

*or hotplate, steamer etc, depending on what sort of bread you make.

 At the start-up phase, when you need to concentrate on becoming a decent baker, you should keep machinery to a minimum. With fewer machines you are going to handle the dough more and intrinsically learn about fermentation and your chosen craft. Later, you can select certain machines that will enhance the output of your already good bread and pastries."

Paul Merry, Panary, Dorset

Basic microbakery bits

While a few of the following items are essential, many are simply useful. Some of this kit might still be of use to a baker who's flown the nest to a bigger bakehouse, but also see the section on larger equipment on page 167.

Baking stone

Opinion on the value of baking on a pizza stone, terracotta tile, granite worktop offcut, or slab of refractory material is divided. Some bakers insist it gives a better oven spring and crust to the underside of a loaf. Others say that, being only a centimetre or two thick, such a stone can't build up enough heat to make any significant difference. They can also take extra time (and therefore energy, money and CO_2) to heat. NB: referring to a loaf produced in a domestic oven as 'stone baked' because it sat on one of these goes against the Campaign's drive for honest marketing.

Baking trays/sheets

The thicker the tray/sheet the better, as thin ones can buckle at higher oven temperatures. Flat ones make it easy to slide off baked products, while those with straight sides are useful for focaccia, tray-bakes etc. Non-stick is fine but can have a limited life when baking frequently. You might find it better to use uncoated steel or aluminium and grease/oil or line it – see below.

Baking tray liners

Instead of using endless amounts of greaseproof paper/baking parchment, you could opt for reusable non-stick sheets that don't need to be oiled or greased and can just be wiped clean.

Banneton

A French word for a proving basket. It holds dough in shape while proving and results in loaves that many bread makers and buyers find appealing – though fashions change, of course. Usually made of wicker or bent cane. Sometimes lined with couche cloth (see below) and/or dusted with flour (a mix of rye and rice works well) to prevent loaves sticking. As they draw moisture from the dough they need to be brushed out and dried thoroughly (eg in an oven after it's turned off and is cooling – remember to retrieve before you turn back on!) between uses to prevent mould growth.

Brotformen

The German version of a banneton, which can be made from wood pulp. It might be more sustainably made than the cane versions and perhaps cheaper. Requires similar care to prevent mould.

Buckets/large jugs

The second key ingredient in Real Bread – water – has to get from the tap to the flour somehow! Having at least a couple of sturdy food-safe buckets will reduce your number of runs to the tap and, hopefully, amount of water sloshed out of bowls or jugs onto the floor.

Casserole dish

Traditional bread ovens hold in steam – and many modern professional bakery ovens can generate it – during the early stages of baking. Steam causes starch at the surface of dough to form a gel. Delaying crust formation allows the dough to expand better during the oven spring stage. Once the steam is expelled, the gel hardens to a glossy, crisp crust. You can approximate this effect in a domestic oven by baking your bread in a casserole or Dutch pot/oven made from cast-iron, aluminium or even glass. Place the dish in the oven as it comes up to temperature, lower the dough in (eg on baking parchment, or thin, reusable baking sheet), put the lid on for the first 10-15 minutes of baking, then remove for the remaining time. This gives good results but isn't very practical or efficient if it limits the number of loaves you can bake at one time, so might not make commercial (or environmental) sense for the microbaker.

Cooling racks

Bread left in or on a tin or tray for more than a few minutes after baking will sweat and go soggy. This isn't nice and can encourage mould growth. Cake racks are fine for limited production but if and when you scale up, you'll end up with them balanced all over the place. Pro bakers use purpose-built trolleys with removable wire shelves.

Couche

Stiff cloth (typically unbleached linen) that can be rucked up into channels to hold softer doughs (eg baguettes and ciabatta) in shape while proving. It can also be used to line some types of proving basket. The cloth can be bought from baking specialists and some general fabric suppliers, and just needs to be shaken/brushed and kept dry between uses to prevent mould growth. It can be tricky to launder as flour gets ingrained and becomes claggy when washed.

Dough scraper

This cheap and simple bit of plastic becomes an extension of many a baker's hand. It can be used to mix and divide dough; lift it out of a bowl or off a work surface; scrape any scraps off bowls, hands, work surfaces and any children (plus some adults) you teach to bake, de-ice a windscreen... Metal versions (eg a 'Scotch') are more durable and particularly good for dividing dough and cleaning hard surfaces, though not so great on wooden ones.

Fridge

Some bakers use a retarder to prove dough at a lower than ambient temperature, for example an overnight final proof of shaped loaves to be baked first thing in the morning - see page 224. A domestic fridge can be used, though not the same one you keep your pet (and own) food in. Capacity and the ability to bring a full load of loaves to holding temperature might be a challenge.

Lame/grignette

A sharp blade can be used to score dough to allow and control expansion during oven spring and reduce the risk of unsightly bursts. Scoring can help differentiate similar-looking breads, add a bakery's signature or simply add an aesthetic flourish. Hand-held razor blades are hazardous - not only risking injury to the baker, they can also get lost and end up in the bread. Using a wooden coffee stirrer as a cheap holder isn't much safer - better to invest in a lame. We, of course, love the Real Bread Loaf Mark-engraved UFO lame handcrafted by Wire Monkey - see page 24. Some bakers prefer using small, very sharp (sometimes scalloped) knives.

Loaf tins/pans

Using tins is more space efficient than making hand-shaped or basket-proved loaves. Choose deep-sided, heavy gauge (ie thick) loaf ones. Always use a release agent to ensure loaves don't stick. Some bakers prefer using hard fat such as vegetable shortening, while others say oil is fine. Pay particular attention to the corners and the neck (ie top part) of the tin. Professional bakers rarely use tins with non-stick coatings as they tend to scratch and peel quickly with frequent use. Clean uncoated tins by wiping clean (or, at most, rinse without detergent) to build up a patina to which the dough is less likely to stick. If a loaf is reluctant to come out of the tin, leave it for a few minutes and steam that's released as it cools may help loosen it. If not, a sharp tap on a hard surface and/or plastic dough scraper should persuade it.

Mixer

When deciding whether to invest in a mixer, you need to weigh up the cost of buying, running, maintenance and repair against how much it will save you in time (ie wages) and how much it will increase the output and quality of your bread and, therefore, potential income. Remember that the size of your oven and number of potential customers are limiting factors - there's no point in forking out for a mixer that will churn out 40kg of dough each time if your oven only holds four loaves, or you only sell 20 loaves a week.

> A larger mixer allows you to create a dough that can be used for more than one type of loaf. This can help ease capacity issues as order volumes increase, without you needing to replace your mixer."
>
> *Ian Waterland, Knead Good Bread, Leicestershire*

Mixing bowl

A three-litre bowl is a good size for up to 1kg of dough. Alternatively, you can mix the dough on a work surface by making a well in the dry ingredients, pouring in the liquid and then incorporating the flour and any other ingredients from the outside edge. For larger batches of dough, you might opt for food-safe plastic storage boxes – see below.

Oven

Microbakers generally start off with what they have at home, be that a gas, electric or even wood-fired oven. The limitations of a domestic oven include capacity (ie how many loaves it will take), maximum temperature, minimal to no heat conducted from the sole (ie oven baseplate on which dough is baked) or radiated from the top and sides, lack of steam retention (especially in a fan-assisted oven) and lack of precise temperature control. That said, most still allow you to turn out a decent loaf. For microbakers looking to expand and improve beyond the limits of their home ovens, small 'semi-pro' ovens are available, such as Tom Chandley's Compacta Pico/Pico Plus, and those made by Rackmaster and Rofco. Working with a wood-fired oven is a whole other book(shelf) and lifetime of learning in itself.

Plasters

Not bakery kit as such, but you should know that, as a food handler, the plasters in your first aid kit need to be blue as they're easier to spot if they fall off.

Proving containers

While a bowl with a lid or other covering is fine for proving a small amount of dough, a plastic food-safe/grade (look for a symbol, such as a glass and fork or (in the USA) Food and Drink Administration approved) storage container with sealable lid makes a good dough trough for mixing and proving larger amounts. A 15-litre container should take about 5kg of dough with space to rise. If retarding dough, make sure your container(s) will fit in your fridge/retarder!

Scales

When baking as a business, accurate scales are essential. They help to ensure consistency of production and that your end products are at the advertised weight. Depending on national or local regulations, you might be required to buy scales that are certified for commercial use, which you may have to have recalibrated from time to time. Professional bakers tend to choose digital/electronic scales.

Shower caps

A number of microbakers have told us how useful these are for covering smaller bowls, rather than single-use plastic wrap/clingfilm. They can be washed and reused many times, if they are good quality ones.

Storage

Lucie Steel, owner of Birch Bread in Berkshire said: "As space is very limited, you may need to store flour elsewhere, such as in a garden shed or garage. Invest in sturdy, watertight and rodent-proof containers that each holds an unopened 25kg flour sack, rather than having to decant it. The flour will keep better and your EHO will be happier, particularly if they're repurposed containers. I bought empty mango chutney drums that have screw-on lids. They're brilliant – durable, washable and so cheap compared to other containers that size."

Thermometers

For greater control of fermentation, a waterproof probe thermometer allows you to check the temperature of water, flour, dough and finished loaves. Checking loaves is a good idea to ensure products are fully baked and might even be required by your local food safety/environmental health officer.

Thermostats on domestic ovens can be inaccurate. Adjusting baking time can offer a successful workaround for plain doughs, but enriched and laminated doughs, cakes, pastries and biscuits tend to be less forgiving. Though you will get used to the hot spots and other quirks of your oven as you bake in it more frequently, a separate oven thermometer allows you to be sure that your oven is at the temperature the built-in thermostat says it is. Some professional bakers use laser thermometers to check temperatures in different parts of their deck or masonry ovens.

It took me a year of trials to produce something saleable from home. Eventually I bought a thermometer and discovered that although my oven said it was reaching 220°C, it wasn't even up to 200°C."

Maggie Rich, Companions Real Bread, Bedford

Timers

Having multiple digital timers is very useful, whether they are reminding you to get one lot of bread out of the oven, fold another batch of dough, or put shaped loaves in the fridge/retarder. Being able to set a different alarm sound for each timer helps when you have several running at once.

Equipment suppliers

The following are just some of the UK companies that supply new (and in some cases used) professional ovens and other bakery kit. Some specialise (eg wood-fired ovens), while others are more general. Please visit the relevant website for details of what each supplies, and our website for any Campaign supporter discounts that they might offer. You can find others on the Real Bread Map.

- Armstrong Brick Ovens www.armstrongbrickovens.co.uk
- Bakery Bits www.bakerybits.co.uk
- Becketts www.becketts.co.uk
- The Bertinet Kitchen www.thebertinetkitchen.com/shop/bread-making
- Brook Food Processing Equipment www.brookfood.co.uk
- Creeds creedsdirect.co.uk
- Mockmill www.mockmill.com
- Nisbets www.nisbets.co.uk
- Panary www.panary.co.uk
- Target Catering Equipment www.targetcatering.co.uk
- Wood-fired Ovens www.wood-firedoven.co.uk

" My advice is to always buy bigger than you think you will need and that tins are your friend! When I first started my microbakery, I baked a lot in tins as I could fit more of them into the oven than loaves proved in bannetons. I didn't offer a lot of sourdough initially as my family got a bit tired of me constantly clearing out the home fridge to load it with dough. The mixer I bought was very old but brilliant and didn't cost much."

Liz Wilson, Ma Baker, London

A note on packaging

When choosing packaging, try to weigh up the positive and negative impacts of its production, use and disposal, against those of other materials. What energy-use, pollutants and other ethical implications are involved? You might think the greenest or most ethical choice is clear-cut but actually glass, paper, cardboard, cotton, hemp, linen, metals, bamboo, bio plastics and every other material all have pros and cons across their life cycles. One might score well on its carbon footprint but badly when it comes to pollutants.

A cornstarch container or film might seem the perfect alternative to plastic, but was it made from genetically-modified corn? How far away was the corn grown and using what agrochemicals? What was the water footprint? Was it grown on land that could have been used for affordable food for local people? What energy, chemicals and pollutants were involved in turning it into something plasticky? Will it biodegrade in domestic compost? What happens when someone puts it in with (ie contaminates) their plastic recycling?

Then there's the paper-versus-plastic bag dilemma. Typically, plastics are made from non-renewable oil/gas or their by-products, don't biodegrade and – though some types are easy to recycle – the vast majority are thrown away, ending up in landfill where they can leach pollutants, or in waterways where they're a threat to wildlife, and break down to micro- and nanoparticles that end up in the food chain.

Paper, then, might seem the obvious choice as it's made from all-natural, carbon-sinking trees or recycled materials, and is easy to recycle or will biodegrade. Paper production, however, has a very high water footprint. It also involves a huge input of energy, so each bag has a relatively high carbon footprint as well, especially considering that most only get used once. Bleaches and all sorts of other toxic substances, which can become pollutants, are used to make or recycle paper pulp.

The weight- and volume-to-strength ratio of paper is typically higher than that of plastic, so you need to use more of it to hold the same amount, creating a greater burden in terms of transportation and disposal. There is also concern that the conditions in landfill sites mean that paper doesn't always biodegrade as quickly as previously assumed, with newspaper, bags and other items being recovered virtually intact many decades after burial.

As an article on the (now defunct) website reuseit.com put it: 'When faced with the question of paper or plastic, the answer should always be neither.'

Even cotton, linen and jute 'bags for life' don't escape criticism. For example, cotton production requires large amounts of land, has a large water footprint, typically involves significant input of (and therefore pollution by) agrochemicals and has a large carbon footprint. Organic cotton production, while lower in agrochemical use, requires even more land and water. However produced, cotton fabric is rarely recycled and various studies have concluded that a cotton bag needs to be used anywhere from over a hundred to many thousands of times in order to offset certain negative impacts down to the level of those of a single-use plastic bag.

It seems, then, that the best option from an environmental/ethical point of view might be for a baker to sell products without packaging and encourage customers to reuse their own bags, containers and (if you sell hot drinks) refillable cups as much as possible. Unfortunately, some local authorities/health departments insist that bread and other food sold in places such as farmers' markets must be packaged, which takes us back to the start of this section... As the jury is very much out, we'll have to leave it to you to do your own research and decide – sorry!

Further reading includes:

'Life cycle assessment of plastic grocery bags and their alternatives in cities with confined waste management structure: A Singapore case study', Ashiq Ahamed et al, *Journal of Cleaner Production*, Volume 278, 1 January 2021

'Plastic, Paper or Cotton: Which Shopping Bag is Best?', Renee Cho, Columbia University's Earth Institute, 30 April 2020

'Comparison of Environmental Impact of Plastic, Paper and Cloth Bags', Kirsty Bell and Suzie Cave, Northern Ireland Assembly, 23 February 2011

'Life cycle assessment of supermarket carrier bags: a review of the bags available in 2006', UK Environment Agency, February 2011

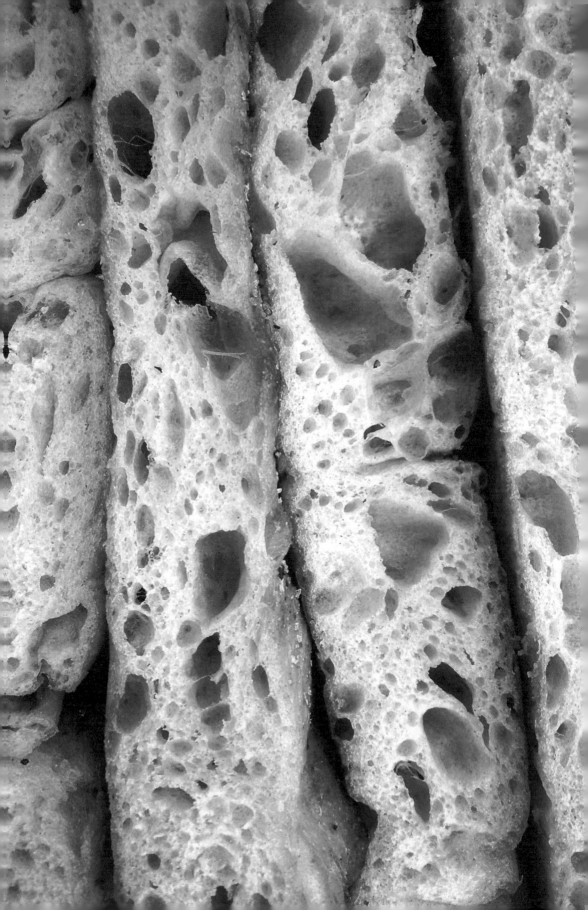

What bread should I make?

The general consensus among bakers we asked was that the beginner should start with just a few types and get really good at them. You might well continue along these lines or branch out from your core range as demand, and your ability to meet it, increases.

> Start with a small product range, rather than aiming to cater for every niche order from the off. When you are confident with your tried and tested products and your muscle memory is firmly in place, you can add new products, which customers love."
>
> *Ian Waterland, Knead Good Bread, Leicestershire*

> For any new product, try making small batches at weekends first – that tends to be when customers are looking for something a bit different. When it starts to sell in larger numbers, extend the production into the weekdays."
>
> *Peter Cook, Peter Cooks Bread, Herefordshire*

Meeting and creating demand

The decision of what to make is yours but you may have to strike a balance between what you want to produce and what people in your area want to buy. You might want to 'educate' or 'teach' people about (we prefer to talk about 'sharing knowledge and pleasure of') types of bread that they aren't used to eating. There's no use in stubbornly baking a mountain of (for example) your favourite 100% wholemeal rye sourdough bread every day if most of it regularly goes unsold and ends up in a food bank or pig trough, though.

If your customers are asking for white sandwich tin loaves, the profitability of your business might depend upon you meeting that demand. In this situation, take pride in making the best white tin loaf you can – which might or might not involve longer fermentation, stoneground flour or other things of particular importance to you.

The bread evangelist in you might get further satisfaction by introducing your passion project breads as specials, even if that's just a handful of those dark rye sourdough loaves each bake day. Give free samples and you might help some people to discover something new they like. Over time, perhaps some will catch on enough to add to your regular range and you might shift the balance.

 We started our service offering seven types of bread each week, including two rotating specials. While this was great for customers it was a nightmare for us as we had to deal with lots of micro-orders each week – sometimes only one person chose a certain type of bread, so we had to make a single loaf just for them. By limiting choice, you keep your batch sizes up and your administration down. As long as your bread is bloody good then most people are very happy with that limited range."

Dan McTiernan, The Handmade Bakery, North Yorkshire

 When I started my microbakery the majority of people in my local community were committed to white and wholemeal tin loaves. At first, only a few people asked if I could bake banneton risen mixed grain sourdough loaves. Over a few years, and with much patient sampling, the market shifted to the point where the tin loaves were the ones that were left unsold."

Jane Mason, Virtuous Bread

More thoughts

- Visit other bakeries in your area, noting their range and prices. Chat to the baker/owner – hopefully you'll find they don't consider you as the competition, but as a like-minded baker who shares their passion for enabling as many people as possible to enjoy Real Bread.
- Have a look at what comparable bakeries further afield are making and selling.
- If you want to introduce new products, only do so one or two at a time, perhaps as specials.
- Keep an eye on national – and even international – trends in baking to see what people are buying. We're not saying follow every new passing fad, but is there something popular that might fit with your ethos, business model and local market?

- Record what is selling well and what isn't and adjust your production accordingly - see the No Loaf Lost section on page 228.
- Offer samples and encourage feedback from your customers.
- Be cautious about allowing an individual customer to dictate your production or distribution. Special arrangements and one-off special requests can be disproportionately hard to accommodate.

> It's important to remember that the bakery business is seasonal. Tracking trends by month over several years will reveal when people are more inclined to buy which products."
>
> *Mark Stambler, Le Pagnol, California*

See also the market research section on page 127.

Not by bread alone

> Nearly five years beyond selling home-made bread, I'm learning that a strong pastry programme can keep a bread programme afloat."
>
> *Mark Stambler, Le Pagnol, California*

There's not much dough in bread: the profit margin isn't large, especially if you are pricing yours to make it as accessible as possible (see page 38). Though some bakeries survive and thrive selling nothing but Real Bread, if you need to supplement your income to sustain your business, things to consider include

- **Cakes, pastries and biscuits** Some people are prepared to pay as much (or more) for a few mouthfuls of a small enriched 'treat' than for a loaf that will provide several meals. If you go down this route, schedule treat baking around your other production, using the oven as the temperature falls after baking bread.
- **Pies, pasties, sausage rolls and other savouries** Again, in many places there is a market for 'grab and go' hot and cold snacks.
- **Sandwiches** Anyone can make sandwiches at home for very little, but some people are more than happy to pay for the convenience of you doing it for them.
- **Coffee, tea and other hot drinks** Similarly, many people are prepared to pay a pretty penny for brown water. Keep it Fairtrade and encourage people to bring their own refillable cups - see note on packaging on page 32.

Might your shop/stall and business model have room to sell food, drink and maybe other items from other local craft/artisanal producers? Selling baking books and kit (eg aprons, scrapers, bannetons, tins etc) might also be an option, particularly if you run classes – see below.

Each of the above will add to your considerations and costs, such as extra skills/ knowledge, ingredient costs, preparation time, space for production and display, and perhaps specialist equipment. There might be tax implications, perhaps VAT/GST or similar being applicable to 'luxury' items where you are. Do your sums (and market research) to assess whether the cost/benefit ratio is likely to work in your favour.

Running classes

Once you have developed your baking and business skills and knowledge, they will have value in themselves. If you have the aptitude, can spare the time and energy, and have or can rent the space, running classes or courses is a way to release/realise this value. If you are at a level where you can run premium-priced classes, please consider also running sessions for people with less/no disposable income. The 'lifestyle' classes can help to subsidise the 'life skills' classes. You might even choose to operate a pay-it-forward system, with people who are able and willing to pay extra helping to fund places for others. As you know, a baking class, or even a short course, alone does not an artisan baker make. Please avoid any temptation to market classes or short courses in a way that could lead people to believe that they'll walk away as an artisan, rather than seeing it as a step in their learning journey.

Bread for all

The Campaign's inclusive vision is for everyone to have the chance to choose Real Bread. In addition to physical/geographic accessibility (ie Real Bread available within walking or cycling distance) an aspect of this mission is financial. How can Real Bread be made affordable for as many people as possible?

Part of the solution that the Campaign and many of our supporters and other friends offer is sharing knowledge and skills to empower and enable people to make bread at home. Another element is our suggested public sector procurement criteria, which we encourage institutions (including schools, nurseries, hospitals, the forces, prisons, as well as some private sector organisations like care homes and work canteens) to use for their catering. Supermarkets and other industrial loaf fabricators could leverage economies of scale and other aspects of their business models to make Real Bread accessible to millions of people, but generally choose not to.

We also encourage all bakery owners and retailers to charge an honest price for an honest crust. Please don't undersell your products or yourself, and be sure to factor in all of your costs in order to maintain a financially sustainable business (see costing and pricing starting on page 75) but also consider what you can do to make your bread affordable/accessible to more people.

While home-based microbakers don't benefit from bulk-buying discounts, or other economies of scale, to the same extent as even a small high street bakery, ingredients account for only a small part of a home bakery's costs. Other than yourself, you have few if any staff costs and your overheads are far lower than if you were paying rent and rates on a prime retail site, buying and maintaining professional equipment and so on.

To be clear, we're not suggesting that micro- or other SME bakeries should try to engage with supermarkets in a race-to-the-bottom price war they won't win. Large retailers are able to perform the neat trick of undercutting small bakeries with lower prices at the till, while still charging a premium for 'artisan style' products and generating large profits and shareholder dividends. Factors enabling them to do so include economies of scale and the ability to use large margins across the rest of the store (and perhaps squeeze suppliers) to more than compensate for any promotions or below-cost selling on some factory loaves. SMEs just can't compete on those terms, nor are you expected to.

Daily bread

The majority of us in wealthy countries have varying degrees of discretion about how we spend our money. Far too many people are in poverty, though. Some have to choose between feeding themselves, their kids or the electricity meter. While organisations including Sustain push for structural change so that more people can afford the essentials, you can play a role in bridging the gap.

You might consider selling a regularly available (be that daily or just on certain days) basic loaf at around what it costs you to produce it. You can use a simple sign or label at point of sale to communicate for whom these loaves are intended - eg people who are unwaged or on low pay. As asking to see evidence of a customer's status can be stigmatising, you might prefer to leave this as an honesty-based system. Some bakeries run pay-it-forward schemes, ie offer customers the opportunity to buy or help to subsidise a loaf for someone else in their local community who's on a tighter budget. Perhaps there's a local charity or community organisation doing relevant work that you can team up with on this.

Hidden costs of 'cheap' food

Ultimately, the solution to food poverty (or rather, just poverty) is largely external to food. Inequalities in income, taxation and benefits are among the root causes of people not having enough money in their pocket to pay for nutritious food, not to mention housing, energy bills, clothing, sanitary products etc.

The long-term answer to poverty can't rely upon making food (and everything else) apparently ever cheaper at the till; it simply isn't sustainable. It is also, at best, sleight of hand: someone, or something, along the line is paying the price – possibly with interest – and you can bet it won't be big business CEOs or shareholders. Displaced costs might include people being paid a pittance and having their working conditions and workers' rights eroded, or losing their jobs in favour of disenfranchised (and even less well paid) workers. Restricting pay and putting people out of work isn't going to help anyone's mental health or lift them out of poverty. Other hidden costs of 'cheap' food can include it being less healthy (or actually unhealthy), which increases the cost of healthcare; losses from local communities and economies; erosion of animal welfare standards; and environmental safeguarding going to hell in a handcart.

Find out more:
» www.sustainweb.org/foodpoverty/whatisfoodpoverty/
» www.sustainablefoodtrust.org/key-issues/true-cost-accounting/

Business planning

If you ever apply for a loan or other form of funding, you'll probably need to write a business plan. Even if you don't, it's worth at least considering the following notes.

Writing a business plan

When (and if) you write a formal business plan is up to you. On one hand you have the old adage, failing to plan is planning to fail. Conversely, Richard 'screw it, let's do it' Branson has written "I didn't really think too much about my first business plan – I just went ahead and did it. It turns out that this was the best thing I could have done. To this day I don't make formal business plans."

A business plan is a description of the enterprise you wish to create. It details your strategy, the vision for your business, the products or services it will provide, its formal structure, your management approach, the results of your market research, and your financial, marketing and human resources plans.

The following points to consider are taken from The Prince's Trust Business Plan pack:

- Who are you, what's your story and what sets your business apart from others?
- What are you going to sell?
- Who are your customers?
- What is the local market like? What will people buy and how much will they pay?
- Who are your competitors and how does your business and your offer compare to theirs?
- How will customers get your bread and will you get paid?
- How much will your business cost to set up and run?
- How much money do you plan to make?
- What if it doesn't work out?

We will look at the first five of these points in the Marketing chapter.

Find out more:

- » www.princes-trust.org.uk/help-for-young-people/tools-resources/business-tools/business-plans
- » www.bplans.com/sample_business_plans.php
- » www.gov.uk/write-business-plan
- » www.the-sse.org/resources/starting/writing-your-first-business-plan/

> " Perhaps most importantly, business planning structures your thinking. If you start from an existing template, of which there are many on the internet and in old-fashioned books, it can reduce the risk of an issue popping up that you really should have considered."
>
> *Ian Waterland, Knead Good Bread, Leicestershire*

> " I think a mission statement and a manifesto are as important as a business plan. Your mission statement sets out what you are hoping to achieve with your business and focuses your mind on this from the outset. A manifesto sets out the principles and ethical boundaries within which you want to operate."
>
> *Romilla Arber, Honesty Group, Berkshire*

> " A good alternative to writing a business plan in narrative format is the Business Model Canvas, which helps you ensure you've thought about every angle of the business. There are lots of freely downloadable versions online."
>
> *Maggie Rich, Companions Real Bread, Bedford*

Business types

Every business is categorised by its legal structure, on top of which you might think of it using an informal description. Factors to take into consideration when trying to decide what type of business yours will be include:

- Why you are running the business.
- Where the balance lies between making a profit and providing affordable food and/or other community or social benefits.

- Whether or not you plan to share the ownership of the business.
- Who should take the financial and legal risks, responsibilities and rewards.

Legal entities

It might feel like a dull or daunting question, but what legal structure do you want (or need) your bakery business to have? Here are some of the more common types for small bakeries to adopt.

Note that under several of these headings we have grouped together similar entities from different countries. Definitions and regulations vary from country to country, and in some cases between localities. The following is a generalised starting point for your own further research.

Sole Trader/Proprietor

This is a business owned and run by one person. It tends to be the least complicated structure for a small food business to adopt. Typically, the business and its owner are one and the same in the eyes of the law and the taxmonster. On the upside it's easy to set up, you have total control and get to keep all the profit after tax. On the downside, you are responsible for all liabilities of the business.

Depending on where you are, as a sole trader/proprietor you might:

- Have to register the business name.
- Have total control over all aspects of the business.
- Make all the decisions regarding investment, funding and products.
- Be entitled to all profits after tax.
- Not have to pay any legal or registration fees.
- Be personally responsible for all debts, losses, liabilities and other obligations of the business, as well as liabilities resulting from actions of any employee.
- Be responsible for paying tax on the profit of the business as part of your personal income.
- Not be permitted to sell stocks/shares in the business and might have difficulty getting a bank loan.
- Not be able to share debts or profits with others, including family members.
- Find it hard to expand or sell the business.

Your personal liability might be unlimited, meaning that a worst-case scenario could be a lawsuit against the company that bankrupts you personally and/or leads to you losing your home. Erm, that looks scarier than it was meant to.

Find out more:
- » www.gov.uk/set-up-self-employed
- » www.mygov.scot/set-up-as-a-sole-trader/
- » www.sba.gov/content/sole-proprietorship
- » www.business.gov.au/Planning/Business-structures-and-types/Business-structures
- » www.canada.ca/en/services/business/start.html
- » www.business.govt.nz/getting-started/choosing-the-right-business-structure/becoming-a-sole-trader/
- » www.citizensinformation.ie/en/employment/types_of_employment/self_employment/self_employment_as_an_individual.html
- » https://supportingsmes.gov.ie/sme-search/

Partnership

This is defined as two or more people trading together as a single business entity. If you decide to run your business with another person such as a friend or spouse, your business will operate with partnership status. This means that:

- A formal partnership agreement covering the responsibilities and rights of each partner should be drawn up by a solicitor. This can also provide details of how the profits will be shared.
- Partners usually share the responsibility for running the business.
- You will be liable for your own and your partner's business debts.
- Each partner pays their own National Insurance contributions and income tax on their share of any profit.
- You do not need to register your business name.
- The process for dissolving a partnership is prescribed in law.

You might choose to give one partner a controlling vote, which will help to avoid any deadlock situations that might otherwise require dissolving the partnership.

As the name suggests, a Limited Liability Partnership (LLP) limits the personal responsibility of partners for any debts and other liabilities the business has.

Cottage Food Operation (USA)

With the exception of New Jersey, every state in the USA has a Cottage Food Law (CFL) that allows people to sell certain foods (usually including plain bread) made in a domestic kitchen. The permissions, restrictions and hoops through which the Cottage Food Operation/Business (CFO/CFB) owner has to jump vary from state to state but limitations/requirements usually include some combination of the following:

- The types of food allowed and/or prohibited – commonly prohibited foods are meat, dairy and fish/seafood, though at least one state prohibits chutney! In some states the rules simply (or ambiguously) say that the food mustn't be 'potentially hazardous'.
- A maximum annual turnover.
- A maximum number of employees.
- Where the food can be sold – often limited to direct-to-consumer retail, such as bake sales, farmers' markets, charity events, producer's home. Most states prohibit indirect sales, such as to/through shops and eateries.
- No sales over the state line.
- No online sales and/or posting/shipping orders.
- The CFO/CFB site and/or operator must be registered and/or licensed or have a permit.
- The owner must complete online (or perhaps in-person) food safety training.
- Inspection(s) of the production site (eg kitchen) and perhaps other parts of the house.
- Food information labelling.

As a 2018 report by the Harvard Law School Food Law and Policy Clinic noted: "Although some cottage food laws are relatively easy to identify and understand, others must be extrapolated from several different state food safety laws that provide unclear guidance. Also, it might be difficult to find a state's cottage food laws because most states do not use the term 'cottage food' in their laws." It's also possible for a county or city to opt out of its state-wide CFL. Contact your local public health department for information and guidance.

Find out more:
- » Cottage Food Laws in the United States, Harvard Law School Food Law and Policy Clinic: www.chlpi.org/wp-content/uploads/2013/12/FLPC_Cottage-Foods-Report_August-2018.pdf
- » Regulatory Guidance for Best Practices: Cottage Foods, Association of Food and Drug Officials: www.afdo.org/resources/cottage-foods-laws-and-guidance/

Co-operative

The International Co-operative Alliance defines a co-operative as 'an autonomous association of persons united voluntarily to meet their common economic, social and cultural needs and aspirations through a jointly owned and democratically controlled enterprise.' Whether or not a co-operative is a legal entity depends on where in the world you are.

In the UK and other places where a co-operative isn't a type of legal entity, you will need to choose one for it – eg a Company Limited by Guarantee, a partnership, Community Benefit Society, Community Interest Company etc. Co-Operatives UK is a useful source of information about establishing a co-operative, the different forms of co-operative, their governance etc.

With the exception of Queensland, the sector is governed across Australia by Co-operatives National Law. Capital is used for the group's common interest, all members have equal status and voting rights, none can hold more than 20% of shares, and each can elect – or nominate themself – as a director.

In Canada, a co-operative is a business organisation owned by the members who use its services. Control is shared equally between members and any profit is shared between members.

In Ireland there is a co-operative legal entity which is an industrial and provident society.

The United States does not have a specific federal law on the establishment of co-operatives, but federal law does apply to co-operatives' tax exemptions. Each state has its own statutes on co-operatives, adding up to about 85 in total, so you'll need to research what applies in yours. The same applies across the EU, where there are at least six models of legislation.

Find out more:
  » UK www.uk.coop
  » Australia www.coopdevelopment.org.au
  » Europe https://ec.europa.eu/growth/sectors/social-economy/cooperatives_en
  » Ireland www.cro.ie/Society-Union/RFS-Industrial-and-Provident-Societies
  » USA www.co-oplaw.org/statebystate/
  » International www.ica.coop

Community Interest Company (UK)

In the UK, a CIC limited by guarantee is a structure particularly suited to social enterprises and not-for-profit businesses. It is a limited liability company that allows some of the freedom, flexibility and other advantages of operating as a business, with some of the checks and balances that apply to charities and mutual benefit societies. This sort of CIC can't be owned by one person or sold on, for example.

Being a CIC may help build the trust of lenders, investors, customers and others that social benefit is at the heart of your Real Bread business, rather than an add-on. A CIC's activity is put on record for public scrutiny and clauses for incorporation include an asset lock that ensures its profits and other assets are used for social/ community purposes, and retention of control by members. Steps for setting up a CIC include:

- Adopting a constitution that meets the relevant regulations.
- Making a declaration that its activities will be carried on for the benefit of the community and how this will be achieved.
- Satisfying the CIC regulator that its activities are indeed for the benefit of the community, rather than just members or employees.
- Excluding itself from political control and a range of political activities.

Find out more:
  » www.gov.uk/government/organisations/office-of-the-regulator-of-community-interest-companies

B corp

Short for 'benefit corporation', a B corp is a legal structure recognised by most states of the USA. A B corp is driven by both financial profit and community/social or environmental benefit. Outside of any legal status, a number of organisations around the world run certification schemes for benefit corporations. They assess the positive and negative impact of a business on its workers, customers, wider community and the environment, with standards for transparency and accountability. The largest of these is run by B Lab, which has certified Hobbs House Bakery in the UK and Grand Central Bakery in the USA, among others.

  » www.bcorporation.net

Other structures

- Private limited company (UK): has one or more shareholders whose liability (eg for financial losses or legal action) is limited.
- Franchise: a company/operator is licensed to trade as a given brand or using a particular name. The brand owner will usually provide training, supply chain, business model and other support for the franchisee.

There are many more, including: Charitable Company Limited by Guarantee, Charitable Unincorporated Association, Charity with subsidiary company, Community Benefit Society, and Limited Liability Company. Carry on with your research and find the one that best fits what you are trying to achieve and how you want to achieve it.

Find out more:
- » UK www.gov.uk/topic/company-registration-filing/starting-company
- » Australia www.business.gov.au/guide/starting   www.jobsearch.gov.au/selfstart
- » Canada www.canada.ca/en/services/business/start.html
- » Ireland www.citizensinformation.ie/en/employment/types_of_employment/ self_employment/setting_up_a_business_in_ireland.html
- » New Zealand www.business.govt.nz/getting-started
- » USA www.irs.gov/businesses/small-businesses-self-employed/business-structures

Informal descriptions

Beyond the legal structure, here are some informal business types that may help you to describe yours. There may be overlap, for example a microbakery might be run as a Community Supported Bakery (see next chapter) in a way that also marks it out as a social enterprise.

Microbakery

Unlike the term small business, microenterprise (aka microbusiness) doesn't have a legal definition in many countries. How one is identified varies around the world. For example, an EU recommendation is that a microenterprise has fewer than 10 employees and an annual turnover or balance sheet below €2 million, while the Australian Bureau of Statistics defines one as having four employees or fewer, but the Australian Taxation Office uses a total business income of less than $2 million (in 2021) as the cut-off. In the UK, the "definitions of small and micro business"

ection of the Small Business, Enterprise and Employment Act 2015 runs to more
han 900 words, but in essence it says that a microbusiness has nine or fewer paid
mployees.

n our experience, what is identified as a microbakery by its owner(s) is typically
 business run by one or two people, often on a part-time basis from a domestic
itchen or other non-traditional bakery setting.

Social enterprise

'or some, the social/community and/or environmental 'capital' generated by a
usiness is as important as the financial one. In some cases it is more important,
vith financial viability simply being a means of perpetuating a social/environmental
nission.

> Our bakery having a positive social impact is definitely more
> important to me than making lots of money. That said, it is
> a financially sustainable base that enables a sustained social
> impact. It is the bakery income that helps fund our aims, which
> are supporting and nourishing the wellbeing of the community
> around us."

Simon Cobb, Stoneham Bakehouse, East Sussex

here is no universally agreed definition of social enterprise. The UK Department
or Business, Innovation and Skills describes one as "...a business with primarily
 ocial objectives whose surpluses are principally reinvested for that purpose in the
 usiness or in the community, rather than being driven by the need to maximise
 rofits for shareholders and owners." The 'Finding Australia's Social Enterprise
 ector' report defined social enterprise as being "...led by an economic, social,
 ultural, or environmental mission consistent with a public or community benefit".

Vhen considering setting up a social enterprise, you should:

- Be clear about the issue/challenge that you want to address, the people you
  want to help and the change you want to help bring about.
- Be able to demonstrate the need for what you plan to do.
- Show how you will help to bring about positive change.
- Decide how you are going to define your aims and measure progress.
- Be able to communicate this clearly and concisely to funders, customers and
  other (potential) supporters.

A social entrepreneur might well have faced – or be working through – one or more of the challenges that their enterprise is designed to address. If you have not, then you should decide how people with that life experience will be involved in the planning and running of the enterprise.

 Having lived it yourself is really helpful in giving your social enterprise some credibility in the early days and gives you a story to work with."

Simon Cobb, Stoneham Bakehouse, East Sussex

Make bread, do good

Missions of some of the social enterprise bakeries in and beyond our network include:

- Employment and life skills training for inside and beyond the prison gate (Bad Boys Bakery and Freedom Bakery, London and Glasgow, UK)
- Training placements for adults distanced from employment by mental ill-health (Better Health Bakery, London, UK)
- Helping people seeking refuge and asylum to shape their lives (Proof Bakery, Coventry, UK; The Bread & Butter Project, Marrickville, Australia)
- Mental wellbeing and growing old gracefully (Planet Leicester Bakers, Leicestershire, UK)
- Helping older people to tackle isolation through getting together to chat and bake bread (Stoneham Bakehouse's BreadShed, Hove, UK)

Sharing work and life skills with women at social and economic disadvantage to help empower them to build a better future for themselves is a mission shared by a number of social enterprises, including Luminary Bakery (London, UK), The Good Loaf (Northampton, UK), Hot Bread Kitchen (New York, USA) and Yangon Bakehouse (Yangon, Myanmar).

The bottom lines

Social enterprises are sometimes described as having double – or triple – bottom lines. In addition to the usual financial column on their balance sheets, they also account for social and/or environmental 'profits' – in some cases assigning monetary values. Social Enterprise International goes as far as encouraging its members to measure up to six forms of wealth creation: natural, human, social, intellectual, manufactured and financial.

Find out more:

» UK www.gov.uk/set-up-a-social-enterprise www.socialenterprisemark.org.uk www.the-sse.org www.unltd.org.uk

» Australia www.socialtraders.com.au www.asena.org.au

» Canada www.secouncil.ca

» Ireland www.socent.ie www.socialentrepreneurs.ie

» USA www.socialenterprise.us

» International www.sei.coop www.socialenterprise.academy/

A partnership led by a Coventry University team created The Social Impact Toolkit to help entrepreneurs understand ways to bring about positive change:

» www.social-impact-toolkit.co.uk

Community Supported Baking

Many a small bakery is embedded in its local community and its owner(s) might justifiably consider it to be a (or *the*) community bakery. Typically, most of its customers will be local people, so you could say the business is supported by the community. We believe, however, that a Community Supported Bakery (CSB) goes further by fundamentally blurring and redefining – or even removing – the traditional separation between the owner and the customers of a bakery business.

 It's not just about having a bakery on the high street for people to go to buy loaves only as and when they need to."

Russell Goodwin, Companio, Manchester

What is Community Supported Baking?

There is no legal, or even generally-agreed, definition of a Community Supported Bakery. The concept echoes Community Supported Agriculture (CSA), which in turn bears similarities to the Japanese teikei system/philosophy. Paraphrasing The Soil Association's CSA definition, we say that a CSB is a partnership between bakers and loaf buyers in which the responsibilities, risks and rewards of running the business are shared. Your own idea of the 'community' in which the bakery thrives might extend beyond bakers and buyers to include cereal breeders and growers/farmers, through to millers, waste warriors and other people in your seed-to-sandwich bread web.

We believe that a true CSB doesn't simply pay lip service to the ethos – for example by running a subscription scheme that only accounts for a small part of the business's turnover. Everyone involved makes a meaningful investment and receives benefits, of one kind or another, as what the Slow Food movement calls 'co-producers'. A CSB might take the form of a worker-owned (or other type of) co-operative or have been crowdfunded and pay dividends to its funder(s). It might be run by a sole trader whose pre-paid subscription orders or bread bonds scheme account for the majority, or all, of its income or starting capital.

A little bit of history

There have always been some bakeries in community ownership. People come together with their neighbours to finance, build, fuel and run a communal oven, with each household having its turn to use the oven. In other cases, someone, perhaps employed by a community collective, bakes dough that people in the neighbourhood have made at home. Over time, such practices disappeared in many countries, though continue in others - Morocco, for example. There also seems to have been a minor revival in parts of the USA and elsewhere with the rise of the communal movement in the 1960s.

We've been unable to pinpoint exactly where or when the current CSB movement began. The first mention of the term Community Supported Baking we've found was by Andrew Whitley, who launched Bread Matters' baking for community course in 2009. The course was attended by (amongst others) Dan and Johanna McTiernan, who later that year launched The Handmade Bakery, which we believe to be the first business to call itself a Community Supported Bakery.

Why set up a Community Supported Bakery?

Benefits for the business might include:

- Investment from within the local community.
- Subscriptions providing predictable demand (and cash flow), also helping surplus reduction.
- Local skills and labour.
- Enhanced social engagement and sense of belonging in a community.
- Greater customer loyalty.

 The bakery has been built on the basis that we would offer local people a genuine alternative to mass-produced loaves and create a real asset for the local community. Judging by our lovely repeat customers, who have become our friends, the growth in the business and numbers of local people we employ, we seem to have achieved that."

Dave Lomax, The Handmade Bakery, North Yorkshire

> Running the CSB has really helped me put roots down in my adopted local community. I know all my customers by their first names, and often their children and pets too!"
>
> *Tom Baker, founder of Loaf, Stirchley*

Depending on the motivations of the people behind a particular CSB, benefits for other people beyond those offered by other types of small local bakery might include:

- Having a stake (monetary and otherwise) in a business that is of real community value.
- A say in how the business is run.
- A subscription guaranteeing there's a loaf with your name on it so that you won't miss out.
- Your investment being repaid – perhaps with interest – in bread or baking classes.
- Subscriber/investor/backer discounts or rewards.
- A pay it forward scheme, enabling customers to buy loaves that the bakery can sell at a lower price (or give) to local people who are unwaged, or otherwise face obstacles to affording delicious, nutritious food.

Investments and rewards

It is useful to decide early on in planning a CSB what type(s) of investment it will ask for and what reward(s) or benefits it will offer in return. The type of relationship people have with the CSB depends upon what those running it need (eg skills, time, knowledge, labour, money, property…) and which of these investments they want to – and can – get from people in the community. It also depends on what the people planning the CSB can and want to offer in return beyond bread – perhaps return on investment, an ongoing stake, skills/training, community space.

Community ownership

Perhaps one of the 'purest' forms of CSB is a worker-owned co-operative. A group of people collectively make decisions about how the bakery business is set up and run. In terms of finance, the group first agrees on the set-up and running costs, including salaries. They then agree how much each member invests (either financially or in kind), how much (and in what form) each will receive in return and what gets reinvested in the business. This approach can be combined with other forms of start-up investment – the members do not necessarily need to contribute to the initial finance. It might well run as a not-for-profit enterprise, with all financial surplus being reinvested in the business and/or its social (or perhaps charitable) aims. See the social enterprise section on page 51 for more.

Capital investment

Setting up and running a larger bakery requires a lot of dough. One way for people to be involved in (and share the financial risks and rewards of) a bakery is to take out shares in, or provide loans to, the business. This might be done through an online crowdfunding (see page 92) or microfinance platform.

In-kind investments

In-kind investments could include waiving/reducing costs of property rental, flour, grain, milling, equipment, labour for fitting out the bakery, shifts running the shop, shifts in the bakehouse, another local business adding bread onto its own delivery rounds, and helping in 'back office' (accounts, ordering and marketing) support.

Bread bonds

Bond holders make a financial investment, then receive their share dividends, interest payments or even (though less likely) repayment of the loan itself in bread or baking classes. This was pioneered in the UK by The Handmade Bakery. The bakery's original bread bond investors received Real Bread as their interest payments, though repayment of their initial capital investment was made at the end of the term of the bond in cash. Breadshare Community Supported Bakery at Whitmuir Farm in Scotland raised funds to buy its first ovens by running a Loaf Loans scheme. This paid interest at an initial rate of 7.5% in the form of bread.

Subscription schemes

One option is that customers commit to, and pay in advance for, a certain number of loaves over a given period of time (eg two loaves per week for three months) rather than ordering and paying on the spot or a week at a time. Bread Bike Community Supported Bakery in San Luis Obispo, California, allows a customers to set up an account by credit card, paying either $40 or $100 at a time. The cost of each order is deducted on a weekly or bi-weekly basis from the account balance until it reaches zero, when another $40/$100 is charged to the credit card.

As well as helping the CSB with cash flow, pre-paid subscriptions give a better idea of demand, thereby eliminating, or at least reducing, the risk of food surplus and waste. In return, subscribers might receive a discount in line with committing to more loaves per week and/or a longer subscription. If the CSB also bakes bread for impulse sales (eg at a farmers' market stall) as an extra stream of income, perhaps the subscriber price is lower.

Payment in kind

People might become co-producers in a CSB by investing their time, skills or knowledge in return for bread or learning new skills themselves. As they are receiving payment in kind, people in this arrangement aren't volunteers and you need to check the implications of relevant employment law. See the section on volunteering starting on page 180.

Laying out your stall

Honest and transparent communication should help you attract supporters and customers. Whatever you decide during the business planning, and then running, your CSB, put the key points down in writing and publish them somewhere visible, like a dedicated page of your website. You might want to present it as some sort of promise or charter. Say what you're doing, why, and how. State your commitments. Make it clear how people can get involved.

Find out more:
  » UK www.communitysupportedagriculture.org.uk
  » Australia and New Zealand www.csanetworkausnz.org
  » Ireland www.communitysupportedagriculture.ie
  » Japan www.1971joaa.org
  » International www.urgenci.net/the-network

Ways to sell your Real Bread

You've done everything legally (and sensibly) required to set up and run a food business, so now you need a way for your customers to get their mitts on your Real Bread.

Three of the most common ways in which start-up microbakers do this are: bakehouse door sales, a market stall and deliveries, either to individual customers or to a shared collection point.

Bakehouse door sales

Perhaps the easiest starting point for the home-based microbaker is for customers to come and collect the loaves from you. This fits in well with a subscription service, or if customers order and pay in advance on a weekly basis, with them then collecting during a specified time slot on your regular bake day.

It should go without saying that your safety and security is paramount and that this option isn't one for all people or in all neighbourhoods. Only go for it if you feel it is right in your situation and consider taking precautions such as:

- Setting the collection time within daylight hours.
- Having a buddy with you during the collection time.
- Only accepting pre-payment - ie no handling cash upon collection.
- Handing the loaves over on the doorstep, rather than inviting customers into your home. You might even keep the chain on if you can squeeze a loaf through the gap.

If you have a shed or some outdoor space, you might instead set up a point from which pre-paying customers can collect their bagged up and clearly labelled loaves. Depending on your circumstances, you might even have an honesty box for people to impulse buy a loaf. If you're handy with wood or metal (or know someone who is) how about making a rack of lockable boxes and giving each regular pre-pay customer a key to collect at a time on bake day that suits them?

Of course, the loaves need to be hygienically kept, protected from the elements and vermin, but it means that you don't have to hang around waiting for people to collect. Then again, some microbakers find that chatting with customers is part of the pleasure and point of the business.

> Subscription and delivery models lend themselves to more flexible working. They can allow a baker to provide freshly baked loaves in time for lunch, dinner or the next day's breakfast, while reducing or completely removing the need for night-time working."
>
> *Ian Waterland, Knead Good Bread, Leicestershire.*

Markets

A farmers', producers' or other local market allows the Real Bread advocate to set out their stall – figuratively and actually. Without the larger overheads and other cons of buying/renting retail space, a market can be a great testing ground for a start-up business. It should also allow you to keep the price of your Real Bread down, making it more affordable to more people. In the longer term, a market offers an extra outlet for your business that takes your Real Bread closer to another group of potential customers.

A market stall can involve a lot of work in terms of supplying, setting up and staffing. As well as the time and costs involved in these, someone will end up standing around for many hours in all weather conditions and demand can be unpredictable. See the No Loaf Lost section on page 228 for suggestions to help minimise the surplus and waste this can lead to.

> One of the other challenges of a market is not knowing what people would buy and whether I would be left with surplus loaves. Visitors to my Friday market tended to be older people, often not wanting to buy a whole large loaf, so I had to adjust my range accordingly to accommodate their needs. I found that there was slightly more profit in selling smaller loaves than larger ones, which led to more efficient oven management as more loaves could be baked on one deck at a time."
>
> *Johanna Bottrill, Jo's Loaves, Luton*

A farmers' market tends to attract people with an appreciation for good food and how it's produced, who are willing to pay an honest price for an honest loaf. Stalls tend to (and, depending on the market organisation and local regulations, might have to) be staffed by people involved in the production of the food they sell, so hopefully you'll be surrounded by like-minded stallholders.

A potential downside is that some people can be excluded from farmers' markets. Prices might be higher than they are willing or able to pay (or they assume this to be the case), they may find it less convenient than a one-stop-shop-any-day-of-the-week supermarket, or generally perceive it's 'not for me'. These challenges also apply to small bakeries and other local shops.

Market organisations

This is a selection of larger organisations that represent markets and stallholders, some of which offer advice and support. There are many other regional and more local organisations.

> » UK www.farma.org.uk www.nabma.com www.nmtf.co.uk www.weareccfm.com www.lfm.org.uk www.fmiw.co.uk
> » Australia www.farmersmarkets.org.au
> » Ireland www.countrymarkets.ie
> » New Zealand www.farmersmarkets.org.nz
> » USA www.farmersmarketcoalition.org

Street vending/trading licences/permits

Away from a licensed market, you might consider getting permission to run a stall in a busy place, such as outside a station or school, at peak hours.

- UK: Unless you are operating the stall on private land, you might need a street trading licence. See page 104.
- Australia: The licence/permit requirement for trading in a street or other public places varies between states. See https://ablis.business.gov.au
- Canada: The licence/permit requirement for trading in a street or other public places varies between municipalities. There might be a waiting list.
- Ireland: You need to apply to your local council for a casual trading licence.
- USA: You might need a Transient Vendor Certificate, which you will be able to find out about when applying for your vendor's licence from the state, county or city as applicable.

Deliveries

If they won't come to you... Delivery allows you to increase sales and accessibility of your Real Bread to customers who can't or won't make the journey to the bakery. How frequent your rounds are depends on demand, your capacity and business plan. If you run a microbakery from home, you might find delivery more convenient than having customers coming to your home. In the case of wholesale, it's more or less a given that you will deliver.

You might be able to deliver to an existing food hub or set up your own shared collection point. Virtuous Bread and Bread Angels founder Jane Mason suggested this might be the staff room at a local school from which teachers can grab their orders, the kitchen at a church or community centre, a pub, or even the home of a customer who's prepared to let you drop off orders for others to collect as well.

 We use local pick-up points where we can. It saves us a lot of time as we can drop off a number of loaves at a community centre, pub, garden centre or whatever for local residents to collect from there. We offer a small incentive to the pick-up point but some won't take this, preferring to do it as their bit of support to our social purpose."

Maggie Rich, Companions Real Bread, Bedford

Downsides of delivery might include staff time and cost; costs of buying or renting, maintaining and running a vehicle; as well as the negative environmental impacts if it runs on fossil fuel.

On yer bike

Bicycles can be a great way of delivering Real Bread, especially in places where you have a lot of customers in a small area. They have far lower purchase/rental and running costs than a van, are much more environmentally friendly, can ride in bus lanes, and can be far quicker in heavy traffic over shorter distances. Disadvantages can include the limit to the number of loaves that you can fit into a bike basket, panniers or trailer; how many drops you can make in a shift; your realistic maximum delivery radius; and the weather (and perhaps pollution) you or your delivery rider might experience.

Chef On A Bike, Dave Foster, said: "You will need to evaluate your delivery routes, the topography of your area and the fitness of both your bicycle and your cyclist. The developments in cycle infrastructure have moved on apace and today many urban areas have designated cycle lanes, often making cycling much quicker than motorised transport for deliveries. Outside city centres, however, is another story. Another factor is other road users. Not everyone always considers the vulnerability of cyclists, so insurance and using bike- or helmet-mounted cameras to record your deliveries are worthy of consideration." He also believes that "using a bike for business is a political choice. You should make your voice heard on developing better and safer travel infrastructure for cyclists, walkers and other road users. Joining Cycle UK, and local pressure groups, promotes the cause and your business."

Emma Parkin, founder of Emma's Bread in Exeter, noted: "Delivering wholesale bread by e-bike into the city centre has saved us thousands of hours of driving stress, to say nothing of the incredibly efficient service that ticks all the boxes in terms of sustainability. We use a local bike delivery company, so they have the headache of fixing the machine and finding riders. They also do all the home deliveries within a certain radius, for which customers are happy to pay."

 We started with an extremely heavy trailer, then upgraded to a Dutch two-wheeler with a custom-built bread box for around 40 loaves. There's never been any looking back. We have now introduced an electric cargo bike into the fleet. The main challenges have been bike quality; we have needed the manufacturers to build bikes extra strong to deal with the loads and conditions. Finding committed riders takes time, but there are heroes out there. Packing the bread takes care and practice. We use large paper sacks as this allows for maximum use of space."

Ben Mackinnon, E5 Bakehouse, London

Van dough

A van increases your delivery capacity and range, though there are costs (financial and environmental) and other considerations to be balanced against these benefits. An electric van is less polluting locally than one running on fossil fuel and the general consensus seems to be that its lifetime carbon footprint should be, in most cases, lower.

In 2010, Colin Hilder of All Natural Bakery shared these thoughts:

- Don't go for cheap, half-dead vans for distribution – they will break down at 4am as the delivery run starts, may be off the road for servicing more often than on it, the servicing costs will be very high and your drivers will hate them.
- Do not use short-term hire or lease vehicles. Look for new or low mileage vans on long rental terms (drive them for 10,000 miles and exchange for a newish

replacement) or on lease with deferred residual payment at end of term.

- Don't permit drivers to contravene parking, Congestion Charge or other traffic regulations, and make this clear to them. If a penalty does come through, pay it immediately to avoid tear-making default penalties or worse. Consider including in the drivers' contracts that after a given point (eg verbal warning for the first incident, written warning for a second) payment of such fines will be deducted from their wages.
- Get loaded and started really early in the morning. If delivering in central London, get in and out before the Congestion Charge applies and traffic gets heavy.
- Use a satnav to set up and optimise your journey routings.

Mobile shop

Falling somewhere between a stall and delivery is a mobile shop, which you can park at different locations. This might be an option if you want to reach out to people right around your local area, perhaps because there are several urban estates or rural villages that are Real Bread deserts, ie with no bakery or other place to buy an additive-free loaf within walking distance.

Although a mobile shop has the negative environmental impact of running a vehicle, it might be lower than that of each of those customers driving to you. Perhaps you could team up with another local producer or food co-operative to increase the range (and appeal) of your offering and help share costs. If considering starting a mobile shop, check with your local authority to see if you need a street trading (or equivalent) licence, and be sure to get the right insurance.

Food co-op

A food buying co-op is a community owned and run enterprise that allows people to enjoy good food at affordable prices, often alongside other health, social and environmental aims. A typical food co-op will operate a farmers' market stall and/or a subscription-based box/bag scheme with collection points and/or deliveries. By operating on a not-for-profit basis, placing bulk orders with suppliers and often relying largely on volunteers, food co-ops reduce the cost to customers while still paying producers a fair price.

In the UK, a number of food co-ops and many more good food retailers, whose focus is also on food producers and the planet, rather than profit, belong to the Better Food Traders network. One could well become your favourite wholesale customer, lacing a regular (and perhaps pre-paid) bulk order with a single delivery point ɔ help make Real Bread accessible to more people, many of whom face financial, eographic, mobility, psychological or other barriers to buying good food.

> We supply 60-80 loaves once a week to our local veg box scheme. They drop about 20 boxes here when they pick up the bread, which their customers then come and collect. Because this has been happening for years, and we have an excellent relationship with them, we give them a special price on the bread, lower than our standard wholesale prices. The benefits are many – it gets our bread delivered out to people who don't live close enough to come to us to buy it, through the packaging people find out about our charity and its work, the scheme promotes events for us via fliers in the boxes, we get business from them when they have barbeques and open days and sometimes we get vegetables at cost price."
>
> *John Forrester, the Blackthorn Bakery, Kent*

ind out more:

» UK www.foodcoops.org
» www.betterfoodtraders.org

Online sales

s the owner of every bakery business of any size, you should really consider aving a website, even if it's just a static page with basic details. Once you have your vebsite, you might choose to offer online ordering through it. This can be as useful o a microbaker with a subscription scheme as it can to a larger-scale wholesale akery owner, particularly if you link it to an online payment/merchant services rovider, such as Sage, Worldpay, Paymentsense or PayPal. No more keeping track of hone and email orders or chasing up payments.

n online shop should include:

* Good quality photos of each product.
* Name and brief description of each.
* Weight and full ingredients list (see the labelling section on page 113)
* Details of where and when the customer can collect their order or have it delivered.

- A clear statement of your order cut-off day and time.
- A simple order form and, ideally, system for payment.

 Online sales saved our business in 2020/21. Without it we would have had a queue for eight hours of the day while we served customers one at a time. Wix was cheap, easy to set up, with a bit of Google Sheets magic helping along the way. We took one photo, wrote a description, put our first loaf online and, without any publicity, customers found our online shop and began ordering within minutes of it going live. You must use a spreadsheet though or it will become a nightmare!"

George Casey, Haddie & Trilby, Warwickshire.

Online sales platforms

These vary from country to country and, in a still developing marketplace, tend to come and go. In 2020, examples of e-commerce tools/sites being used by UK bakeries in our network included:

Goodtill/GoodEats Offers a range of tools for online and point-of-sale retail for food and drinks businesses.

NeighbourFood Is basically an orders-only farmers'/producers' market. You sign up as a producer for a local market. Shoppers order online to pick up from the collection point on the set date.

Open Food Network Allows businesses to take online orders and arrange home deliveries. Some bakeries set up their own online shopfront, others work with other local producers to set up food hubs and/or sell through the national network of shopfronts already trading on OFN.

PayPal Love it or hate it, the company offers a shopping cart system that can plug straight into most existing websites. You need some technical knowledge, but it includes a full payment system, stock control etc.

Shopify Says it's: 'The all-in-one commerce platform to start, run, and grow a business.'

Social media

If you don't have an online ordering system, a workaround that works for some microbakeries is using a social media account to post details of the next bake and invite customers to email their orders by a certain date and time. You then reply to advise details of payment and collection or delivery.

Insurance

When you are in business you need insurance. Depending where in the world you are, certain types of cover might be required by law. Others are just sensible to cover your liability for something going wrong, which will minimise the negative financial impact on your business, yourself and others. An insurer might also provide advice and assistance clearing up the mess.

If you are running a microbakery from home, your existing car, property and contents insurance might not be sufficient. You might be able to get an extension or need to take out new or separate cover. Key areas of cover you might want – or need – to take out include:

Public liability

This cover protects you if someone other than an employee is injured, or their property is damaged, because of your business. Perhaps someone slips over in your shop, cuts or burns themselves in a baking class you run elsewhere, is hit by your market stall blowing over, or your oven blows up and knocks out a neighbour's windows.

Product liability

Of course you're never knowingly going to sell a dodgy pork pie, but you still need cover for the minimal risk of someone getting ill after eating one of your products.

Employer's liability

In the UK and in some other territories, a business that has one or more employees is legally required to have this cover. It protects an employee, and you/your business, if they are injured at work.

More cover

Depending on the size, type and location of your business, other areas you might need/want to cover include:

- Buildings and contents.
- Engineering failure.
- Theft.
- Cash (eg while running a market stall).
- Goods in transit – such as a vanload of loaves damaged during delivery.
- Business interruption.
- Motor vehicles – breakdown, injury to the driver and third parties.
- Legal expenses.
- Equipment/tools.
- Stock (if not covered under contents).
- Personal injury and accident.
- Income protection.
- Trade credit insurance: covers a customer not paying debts on time, or at all.
- Private medical insurance.
- Life insurance.

Shop around

Look into, and contact, different insurers to see which offers the most suitable option for your business, striking the right balance of price and cover that you need. Some companies offer policies specifically aimed at bakeries, home-based food businesses, and even home baking businesses. If there isn't an off-the-peg policy that hits the mark, an insurer might tailor one for you. Going through a broker might help, or you might find a bakery or other trade organisation that has an arrangement with an insurer to offer its members an exclusive, or discounted, policy.

Places to find information on business insurance cover requirements and insurers include:

- » UK www.abi.org.uk
- » Australia www.insurancecouncil.com.au
- » Canada www.ibc.ca
- » Ireland www.insuranceireland.eu
- » New Zealand www.icnz.org.nz
- » USA www.namic.org

Money matters

Spending, baking and making dough is an ongoing cycle. If you're just starting out as a small business, check with your local authority to see if they run, or can point you towards, business information sessions. If so, these may include information on tax, banking and so on, and they may offer training sessions on bookkeeping and all matters financial.

As a bread baker, you make bread. When you own a bakery, you work with spreadsheets, so need to become equally adept with them."

Mark Stambler, Le Pagnol, California

Costing and pricing

Getting this right can be tricky. Charge too little and you'll run at a loss, making your bakery unviable as a business. At the other end of the scale, you could set prices that exclude people in your community from buying your Real Bread and you might even price yourself out of the market of people who can afford it.

Why are you doing this? It's a hard question that needs an honest answer. Is it just to get covered in flour every day? If so, fine but make sure you are taking care of the money, or it could become an expensive hobby."

George Casey, Haddie & Trilby, Warwickshire

Calculation

Sticking your finger in the air and thinking of a number is not the best idea. The same goes for basing your prices purely on what other bakeries charge. Neither your costs or what you make will be exactly the same and they might've got their sums wrong, anyway. It makes business sense to set your prices based on your own actual costs and target profit margin.

The most accurate way of costing an item is to calculate all of the direct costs of putting it on the shelf and then apportion a percentage of all of your other business costs to it. You then price the item by multiplying the cost price by your target profit margin.

As a small business owner, you might well find that a spreadsheet (either one you create yourself or find from a reputable source online) is all you need to do the calculations. For larger businesses, software is available with all sorts of functions, including costing and pricing.

For each product type:

a. Multiply the cost per kilo of each ingredient by the amount you use in each loaf/piece, then add these together.

b. Calculate the active production time (ie not including proving, baking and other time when the baker can be doing something else) spent making a batch, multiply by the hourly rate of the baker(s) involved, then divide by the number of units in the batch.

c. Work out the units of energy used to bake the batch, multiply by the cost of a unit of energy, then divide by the number in the batch.

d. Calculate the monthly average total of all of your other costs (see below) and apportion an amount of this.

e. Add together all of the above and multiply by your target profit margin.

If bread of one size is all you make and sell, you might do this simply by dividing all of these costs by the monthly average number of loaves you sell. Otherwise, you'll need to decide how much each unit of each product type will contribute towards covering your costs. A spreadsheet or bakery software programme will allow you to tweak your numbers up and down until you're happy with the split.

Ignoring the importance of costing up all products and pretending that you are making cash is a simple way to lose all the money that you have earned."

George Casey, Haddie & Trilby, Warwickshire

Creating your own spreadsheet has the advantage of you understanding how and why it functions. It will of course need thorough testing!"

Ian Waterland, Knead Good Bread, Leicestershire.

Other costs

Sit down at a keyboard (or with a piece of paper) and note down all of your other outgoings across the year. One set will be salary/wages (including your own) for time spent on activity other than the production you factored in above, such as serving customers, cleaning, admin, management and deliveries.

Depending on the type and size of your baking operation, they might also include:

- Other staff costs, eg national insurance, sick pay, parental leave, benefits.
- Insurance.
- Business rates.
- Bakery rent or mortgage.
- Market stall pitch charge.
- Equipment and vehicle cost and depreciation. What is a realistic time period over which to spread each of these costs? How long do you intend to use your oven mixer or van before selling it on? How much will you then be able to sell it for?
- Maintenance, repair and replacement. What is the average you are likely to spend per year?
- Waste disposal charges.
- Loan repayment.
- Water rates.
- Cleaning materials.
- Professional services – eg accountancy, marketing, web design etc.
- Do you want to set up a 'rainy day fund' to tide the business over in case your sales forecasts turn out to be optimistic or for an unexpected sharp drop in business, as happened for many in 2020/21?
- Contingency – do you want to put an amount each month into an emergency fund for any unforeseen major expenditure that won't be covered by insurance, or that you have to pay upfront and then claim back?
- Packaging (all of those paper bags, coffee cups and so on add up...)
- Fuel costs, if using a motor vehicle for delivery.
- Energy costs/bills other than baking and proving.
- Wastage – the full cost price (not just ingredient cost) of all products you give or throw away. Ideally this would be zero but realistically you will generate surplus and waste, so need to factor it into your costings. See the No Loaf Lost section on page 228.

Target profit

Deciding your margin is mainly a question of how much you want to make over and above what you need to charge to cover your costs.

- While not all benefits are monetary, is there a particular level of financial return you want for the amount of time, effort and self that you are investing?
- How much do you want/need to put away to invest in the future of your business?
- If you have staff members, do you want to set up a profit-sharing bonus scheme?
- Do you want to run on, or close to, a break-even basis in the interests of affordability/accessibility?

As with apportioning your costs, unless you only bake one size and type of bread, profit is best set by product or product category, rather than as one percentage across everything you sell.

 We aim for a 60%-90% gross profit (GP) on all products we make. Calculating the daily and weekly GP against sales is essential to really know how you are doing. Get a GP calculator app to help work this out or become a spreadsheet wiz. Once you get into the habit of recording figures it is easy to continue. It gives you confidence that you are doing well or kicks you up the bum if you need to cut back on the truffle and caviar bread."

George Casey, Haddie & Trilby, Warwickshire

Other pricing considerations

Be prepared for a bit of trial and error, tweaking prices as you are getting established. Initially, it might pay to err towards the higher end of what your calculations and research suggest is the right ballpark. Unsurprisingly, customers are likely to be happier if you manage to drop your prices than if you have to put them up.

Perceived value and worth

What value do you and your potential customers feel you have added to that mixture of relatively inexpensive ingredients? How much are people able and willing to pay? In one place, people might think nothing of paying a premium to have a high-quality loaf gift-boxed and delivered as a luxury gift instead of flowers or wine. In another location people may consider Real Bread priced at little more than an industrial white sliced loaf to be a 'rip off', even if they can afford it. In many places, of course, most people fall somewhere in between these extremes. It pays dividends to do your research and get your marketing messages ready before you open.

Don't be tempted to get into a price war with a nearby supermarket, chain bakery or other larger operator with deeper pockets who benefits from economies of scale. You will lose. Remind yourself that not all loaves are created equal and, like when playing Top Trumps, base your marketing on the categories in which you score highly. See the Marketing chapter for inspiration.

> Real Bread bakers' biggest competitors are those places packed with people walking around aimlessly attached to metal trolleys and baskets. It is worth remembering you cannot win the price war with those guys, though. Many have tried and failed badly. Be different and be better. Price isn't as important as the emotional connection you may be lucky enough to create with your customer base. Though people buy from people, the product really needs to be exceptional, which can take time to achieve."

George Casey, Haddie & Trilby, Warwickshire

What is your mission?

Is one of the reasons that you run a microbakery to make Real Bread affordable to as many people as possible? If so, how do you fit this in with all of the above? Maybe you can set a lower margin on one or more everyday staple breads and a higher margin for luxury/discretionary products such as pastries, cakes and hot drinks. Maybe those higher margin products could even help to subsidise your everyday Real Bread. See notes on page 39.

Whether or not you intend or even realise it, your pricing is an element of your brand identity. It is a factor in a person's perception of whether or not your bakery and they are meant for each other.

Alternatives

If the above all seems too complicated, there are other options. You might take inspiration from some food service (restaurant, food truck etc) operators, who simply calculate menu prices by taking the cost of ingredients per portion and multiplying it by a factor of around three or four to account for all of their other costs and profit margin. As the cost of bread's basic ingredients (flour, water, yeast, salt) is just pence/cents per 100g, you might well need a higher multiplication factor. Keep an eye on your sales and balance sheet to be sure you're in the right ballpark.

Banking

No matter how small your business, you will need to keep your personal finances separate from your business finances. Operating an independent business account allows you to do this. It is also of great benefit for your income tax records. You should plan ahead to have your account fully operational before you start trading.

Adding an additional account under your name is straightforward with most high street banks. All banks should be able to provide an information pack on starting a new business. Some include business planning and finance software. Most banks will show you how to keep a simple set of accounts. A benefit of approaching the local branch of a bank is (or at least should be) the value of their local knowledge. Staff members will often know the locality, the people and often the market possibilities within your area.

Ethical banking

When you pay money into a bank, building society, credit union etc it doesn't just sit in a vault, it gets invested. Whether or not there's any such thing as 'clean money' is a moot point, but some financial institutions have ethical policies in place to prevent them from investing in (for example) the arms trade, fossil fuels, animal testing or investments linked with human rights abuses; or from avoiding corporate tax and lending to iffy governments. Organisations such as Ethical Consumer can help you ask questions, know what to look out for and navigate your way to one that best aligns with your values.

Find out more:
» www.ethicalconsumer.org
» www.ussif.org
» www.gabv.org
» www.banktrack.org

How much!?

If you are challenged about your prices by someone who apparently/clearly has disposable income and discretion about how they spend it, here are some points that could help you to respond.

As the owner of a small, local Real Bread bakery, you might well need to charge more for a loaf than an industrial loaf fabricator or multiple retailer. You don't benefit from the same economies of scale. The cost of ingredients per unit will be higher. Fixed costs have to be split between fewer sales. In short, you're unable to 'pile 'em high, sell 'em cheap.'.

In the case of an SME bakery with staff, the business helps to sustain more jobs per loaf than larger companies, for which we advocate paying a fair, living wage. The money spent with a small independent business that helps to keep a high street alive is more likely to be invested locally (than, say, slip into the pockets of a national business's fat-cat shareholders), supporting the region's economy.

As we often say: not all loaves are created equal! It is not appropriate to attempt making a price comparison between Real Bread handcrafted by a genuine artisan baker and an additive-laden product churned out by a factory. In addition to the higher price of ingredients – perhaps on account of being higher quality and/or from a small supplier – there is value in the artisan baker's knowledge and skills.

How much is this person willing to pay for something that will be gone in minutes – a takeaway coffee, beer, glass of wine, sandwich, cake or pastry, for example? How does that compare to the price of a delicious, nutritious, high quality loaf of Real Bread that they can enjoy across a number of meals?

It's also possible to direct the price question at factory loaves. How can a supermarket justify charging perhaps 80-100% more for its 'standard' loaf than for its own-brand 'basic' white loaf, and maybe around two-and-a-half to three times as much for its 'premium' version? All three will be the output of CBP manufacturing (see page 10), with similar (or identical) ingredients, additives and production costs. How can the retailer justify charging a premium for an 'artisan' loaf if it did not benefit from, or help support the job of, an artisan baker?

Tax

If the old adage is to be believed, tax is one of only two certainties in life. We only scratch the surface here, and as your business grows and evolves, you will need to keep abreast of your obligations.

UK

If you start working for yourself, you must register with Her Majesty's Revenue & Customs (HMRC) as self-employed (sole trader), even if you already send in a tax return. Even if you're not paying tax, if you fail to register within three months of self-employment, you could be liable to a fine. You will start paying income tax on your business's profit once it goes over your personal allowance.

HMRC offers a range of courses and other guidance on income tax and National Insurance. These include free, local workshops designed for people who are starting, or about to start, self-employment. HMRC also offers a one-to-one service to discuss any difficulties you may be having.

Find out more:
» www.gov.uk/browse/business/business-tax

Australia

A sole trader (see business types on page 45) can apply for an Australian business number (ABN). You'll be taxed at the individual income tax rate, with the same tax-free threshold. You may be eligible for the small business tax offset. You must lodge an annual tax return, then will receive a notice of how much you owe by when. If your income goes over a certain amount, you'll be taxed in Pay As You Go instalments instead. A business partnership:

- Must apply for an ABN.
- Must be registered for GST if its annual turnover is above the relevant threshold.
- Shares income and losses between the partners.
- Has its own Tax File Number.
- Must lodge an annual partnership return showing all income and deductions.
- Doesn't pay income tax on its profit. Instead, each partner reports their share of the partnership income in their own tax return and pays tax on their share of the partnership profit at the individual tax rate. Partners may be eligible for the small business tax offset.

f you run a not-for-profit organisation, you might be eligible for tax concessions.

Find out more:
>> www.ato.gov.au/Business/Starting-your-own-business

Canada

As a sole proprietor, you pay personal income tax on the net income your business has generated. You have sole responsibility and assume all risks and gains of the business. You will need to fill out a T2125 (Statement of Business or Professional Activities) form to calculate your business income. You then report your total income and expenses on a T1 personal income tax and benefit return form. You might have to pay by instalments and may also need to make CPP (Canadian Pension Plan) contributions on your own income. You may have to register for GST if your income exceeds the threshold.

A partnership doesn't pay income tax on its profit or file an income tax return. Instead, each partner reports their share of the partnership's income and losses on their own tax return and pays tax on their share of the partnership profit at the individual tax rate. The partnership will also have to file a Partnership Information Return (T5013) form if its absolute value is above the threshold.

Find out more:
>> www.canada.ca/en/services/taxes/income-tax
>> www.canada.ca/en/revenue-agency

Ireland

When setting up as a sole trader, you need to inform Revenue using form TR1. You are responsible for the payment of your own tax and Pay Related Social Insurance (PRSI) and Universal Social Charge (USC). You need to register for a Personal Public Service Number (PPSN) from the Department of Employment Affairs and Social Protection. You also need to register as self-employed and for Income Tax (IT) with Revenue.

If your business is not incorporated, you will pay tax under the self-assessment system once a year. You must pay Preliminary Tax (an estimate of tax due for your current trading year), as well as make a tax return for the previous year. You must keep records that include all purchases and sales of goods and services and all amounts received and all amounts paid out. If you are working from home you may be able to claim a proportion of household bills.

If you set up a business partnership, you (or your tax agent) must inform Revenue. If you do it yourself, you need to complete a Form TR1. You can use this to register for: Income Tax, Employer Pay As You Earn (PAYE), VAT and Relevant Contracts Tax.

If you start a new company, you need to apply to the Companies Registration Office for a CRO number. You (or your tax agent) then must inform Revenue. If you do it yourself, you need to complete a form TR2. You can use this to register for the above taxes. If you start a limited company you can do so yourself via the CRO or with the assistance of your accountant.

Find out more:
> www.revenue.ie
> www.citizensinformation.ie/en/money_and_tax/

New Zealand

As a sole trader, you will pay tax on net profit by filing an annual individual income return (form IR3) using your personal IRD (Inland Revenue Department) number. If you set up another type of business (eg company or partnership) you need to apply for a separate IRD number for it. In either case, you need to submit details of your income for the tax year and of any business activity expenses you want to claim, using the relevant form - eg form IR4 for a company tax return.

A partnership files its tax return every year (form IR7) and can claim any business expenses it incurs. Income is shared among the partners who then each pay income tax according to their shareholding (and, therefore, income) under their personal IRD numbers.

If the partnership agreement allows a partner to take a salary or wage, they will have Pay As You Earn (PAYE) tax deducted from this pay. The partner can then claim PAYE as an expense in their individual tax return. If you had to pay more in tax than the current threshold at the end of the year, you will have to pay provisional tax in instalments during the following year.

Find out more:
> www.ird.govt.nz/income-tax-for-business
> www.business.govt.nz

USA

If you start working for yourself, you must register with the IRS under self-employment (SE). Your SE payments contribute to your coverage under the social security system, which includes retirement benefits, disability benefits and hospital insurance. If your earnings from your SE business are above the threshold, you must pay SE tax and file Schedule SE (form 1040). To figure out net earnings from self-employment you need to use Schedule C or C-EZ.

A business partnership (see business types on page 46) files with the IRS accordingly. One partner must file an annual information return that reports income, deductions, gains, losses etc. A partnership doesn't have to pay income tax. Instead, it 'passes through' any profits or losses to the other partners. Each partner includes their share of the partnership's income or loss on their own tax return.

Find out more:
   » www.irs.gov/businesses/small-businesses-self-employed

Sales tax

UK

Food and drinks (including bread, cold sandwiches for takeaway/delivery, tea/coffee, cakes, pastries and some biscuits) are usually zero-rated for VAT. Items that are standard-rated include (but are not limited to) savoury snacks, hot food for takeaway/delivery and soft drinks. If you run an eatery, you must charge VAT on everything eaten and drunk on the premises.

If your VAT (Value Added Tax) taxable turnover for the previous 12 months is more than the current threshold (£85,000 for 2021/22) or if your business will reach the threshold in the next 30 days, you must register for VAT. If taking over an existing business, you have to add your own VAT taxable turnover over the last 12 months (if any) to that of the business you're taking over. If the total goes over the registration threshold on the day of the takeover, you will have to register for VAT. You must then charge the right amount of VAT, pay any VAT due to HMRC, submit VAT returns, keep VAT records and a VAT account.

If you begin trading before registering for VAT, you cannot charge it. After you register, you should consider increasing your prices to account for the VAT you will have to pay and letting your customers know why, rather than it coming from your profits.

Find out more:
- » www.gov.uk/topic/business-tax/vat
- » www.gov.uk/guidance/rates-of-vat-on-different-goods-and-services

Australia

Goods and services tax (GST) is charged on most goods and services. There are many exemptions for food sold cold for consumption off the premises, but there are many variations even under what can be categorised as bread and baked goods. For example, most bread is exempt, while croissants are not; bagel chips and crostini are exempt if they are baked, but not if they are fried; and a baguette is only exempt if it isn't sold filled. You must register for GST if your business or non-profit organisation has a GST turnover above the current annual threshold ($75,000 and $150,000 respectively in 2021). To register, you will need an Australian Business Number (ABN). You have to collect this extra money (10% of the sale price in 2021) from your customers and then pay this to the Australian Taxation Office (ATO) when it's due.

Find out more:
- » www.ato.gov.au/Business/GST
- » www.business.gov.au/registrations/register-for-taxes/register-for-goods-and-services-tax-gst

Canada

A business has to register for, and pay, the Goods and Services Tax (GST) and the Harmonized Sales Tax (HST) when it exceeds the revenue threshold ($30,000 in 2021) in a single quarter, or cumulatively across four consecutive quarters. Most basic groceries (including bread) are zero rated for GST/HST but tax applies to other foods and drinks, including most snack foods, cakes and many other baked goods that are either sweetened or have a sweet coating or filling. The Canada Revenue Agency website has a list. You must file a GST/HST return even if you have no business transactions and/or no net tax to remit. GST is not charged on bread but it is charged on pastries if they are sold individually ready to eat. Pastries sold in packs of six or more to take home, however, are exempt from GST.

Find out more:
- » www.canada.ca/en/revenue-agency/services/tax/businesses/topics/gst-hst-businesses.html

Ireland

According to the Revenue (Irish Tax and Customs) website, generally, you must register for VAT (Value Added Tax) if you are an accountable person. An accountable person is a taxable person (for example, an individual, partnership, company) who supplies taxable goods or services in the State and is registered or required to register for VAT. A taxable person is any person who independently carries out a business in the European Union (EU) or elsewhere. It includes persons who are exempt from VAT. Registration is obligatory when your turnover exceeds, or is likely to exceed, the VAT thresholds in any continuous 12-month period. You submit a VAT return every two months and pay Revenue the difference between VAT you collected and VAT you were charged.

Find out more:
  » www.revenue.ie/en/vat

New Zealand

Goods and Services Tax (GST) at a rate of 15% (2021) is collected on most goods and services. You will need to register if your annual turnover exceeds NZ$60,000 and/or you add GST to your prices. Most small businesses choose to file two-monthly or six-monthly GST returns, though the latter is not always available if your turnover is less than NZ$500,000. For sole traders your GST number will be the same as your Inland Revenue (IRD) number. When completing your GST return you will need to know your total sales and income, your total spending, including purchases and expenses, and total amount of GST you've charged to customers. You can register for GST when registering your company through Companies Office.

Find out more:
  » www.ird.govt.nz/gst

USA

Retail sales tax at point of purchase of goods and services is imposed by most states and Washington DC. While most states don't impose tax on the sale of basic groceries, many do tax 'prepared foods'. If you live in a state that does tax food sales, as a business owner you are required to assess and collect sales tax. You might also need to obtain a permit to do so. You then need to complete a sales tax return, usually monthly or quarterly, with the appropriate authority. Rates vary over time and from place to place, as does what is taxable, and how often and how you file and remit sales tax. Check with your local authority.

Find out more:

» www.irs.gov/businesses/small-businesses-self-employed/state-government-websites

Taking payment

In order to maximise sales and provide great service to your customers, you need to offer payment methods that best suit the majority of them. You then need to balance this against the costs and other challenges to you of accepting each type, and of the extra accounting and admin time of having multiple types.

Options include:

- Cash
- Mobile card readers
- Online payment platforms
- POS credit/debit card payment machines
- BACS
- Merchant credit/debit card account

Cash

While card (increasingly contactless) payments have overtaken cash in the UK and elsewhere, or are on the way to doing so, many people still prefer using good ol' coins and notes – particularly for smaller transactions.

- Always ensure you have a cash float, record how much it is and (preferably) checked by two people at the start and end of the day/shift.
- Count the money taken at the end of the day/shift and record this. This should then be double-checked, ideally by a second person.
- When counting cash, you need a secure space with a surface on which to count and bag up the money, away from the view of customers.
- Banks require coins to be bagged up according to the denomination and value specified on their bags.
- Pay your takings into the bank as soon as possible, so that they appear both in your financial records and on your bank statement on the same date.
- If you're unable to pay the money in straight away, make sure you have somewhere secure to store it, such as a lockable cash box or safe.
- If applicable, set aside a petty cash float from which payments should be made, rather than directly from cash received.
- If a supplier insists on payment in cash, ensure that you get a receipt.

Mobile card readers

Since the original edition of this book, there has been a proliferation of mobile credit/debit card readers and service providers. The machines connect via Bluetooth to a smartphone or tablet running a merchant service provider's app, which transfers the funds directly to a bank or online payment account.

Mobile card readers allow traders to take payments anywhere with a strong enough phone signal, and make it simple for the customer to tap a card, insert it and enter a PIN, or (in some cases) make a mobile payment using a smartphone or other device. The packages on offer tend to have an initial set-up cost but are then contract-free, with the merchant service provider keeping a small percentage per transaction. Others offer the option of reducing/eliminating transaction fees by paying a monthly charge instead.

At the time of writing, merchant service providers include: iZettle, PayPal, Shopify, Square and SumUp. Some offer detailed sales tracking reports and extensions/ integrations such as online payroll and marketing services. Providers, rates and everything else to do with mobile card readers are in constant flux, so you'll need to do your research to find current details and find the one that will work best for you and your business.

Other card readers

In an odd use of the term, what are known as 'traditional' card readers are similar to mobile ones but tend to be larger and rely on a WiFi connection. Again, advantages, disadvantages and fees vary between systems and providers.

Online payment platforms

These include Braintree, Handepay, PayPal, Sage Pay, Shopify, Square, Stripe, takepayments and Worldpay. Typically, they can be integrated with your bank account and, if you have one, card payment system. Fees can vary greatly and each has pros and cons, so ask around and shop around.

Merchant credit/debit card account

Rather than get your personal and business finances tangled up, it's wise to keep them separate. Your bank will also be able to provide advice, but when setting up a business account it is wise to shop around to compare their rates (fees and interest) and the type and level of support each will provide.

Bread and barter

It's unlikely that exchanging loaves for other goods or services could form the basis of a sustainable business model – though if you do succeed, please let us know how! It might, however, be part of what you do that helps build and strengthen connections with other people and businesses in your area.

Some possibilities:

- **Ingredients** The Thoughtful Bakery in Bath sometimes offers discounts in exchange for ingredients that can be used in the bakery, which customers have grown, gleaned or foraged.
- **Liquid bread** Might a local pub swap a few pints of ale (for you to use in baking, of course...) for bread for their menu?
- **Space and facilities** Could you use bread to pay (at least in part) for these? Eg you use a restaurant's oven when they are not, in exchange for loaves for their menu.
- **Labour** Giving bread as part of staff pay doesn't really work but you might offer it as a benefit on top of their salary.

NB In the UK, at least, giving bread to volunteers in thanks for their help is a no-no as it can be seen as payment – see page 181.

 My colleague negotiated the purchase of a board table and chairs from the ReUse Centre next door for three pizzas!"

Maggie Rich, Companions Real Bread, Bedford

Taking payment as a wholesaler

From his experience running a number of bakeries, Troels Bendix suggested:

- Be strict with your credit terms.
- Set out your terms and conditions of sale and credit clearly and get each customer to sign an agreement.
- Do not be afraid to withhold supply if a customer breaches the agreed terms.
- Encourage electronic payments but accept all kinds of payment.
- When you open your bank account, look for one with a long free banking period and ones with low/no charges for depositing cheques and cash.

Collecting cash on delivery is good for the customer and for your cash flow but, as Colin Hilder noted, it can delay the driver, has to be held somewhere safe until it can be banked, and might incur higher bank charges.

The consensus seems to be to avoid agreeing to any sale-or-return arrangements.

Accounts and other administration

You need to have good administrative systems to keep records of orders you have placed with suppliers, orders you have taken, sales, and also contact details for customers.

There are a variety of systems that you could use including:

- Paper-based systems.
- Computer systems (eg Excel, QuickBooks, Microsoft Office invoice templates).
- Web-based databases.

Paper

Advantages: simple, cheap, doesn't need access to a computer or any technical knowledge.

Disadvantages: difficult to create a backup copy (other than carbon paper or making photocopies), time consuming, calculations have to be done manually, takes longer to send to another party (eg your accountant), and harder to update and make corrections.

Computer

Advantages: the data is in a standardised format, easy to email to others, easy to cut and paste information from other spreadsheets eg previous accounts or catalogues from suppliers, can be used to perform a variety of calculations as well as storing information.

Disadvantages: you need to have a computer, buy a copy of the software and have some IT skills, although spreadsheets are relatively easy to use.

Web

Having a web-based database allows your customers to place their orders and pay online. Most web-based systems will manage all finances as well as customer details and orders and also have other functions such as enabling you to print off invoices. This sort of system is good if you have large numbers of customers and also if you have several different outlets or multiple drop-offs.

The main advantage is that all your orders will be handled by one system rather than lots of different spreadsheets and databases. Also, if designed well, they are generally easy to use.

The main disadvantage is that anyone using the system needs to have internet access. There is also always a cost whenever a payment is made on-line, as payment systems like PayPal charge a fee per order and a percentage of the cost. Therefore, a pay online facility is really only cost effective if you are taking a lot of orders. However, it is also possible for people to order online but still pay by cash, cheque or standing order. A web-based system may also cost quite a lot to develop and there will be an ongoing web hosting cost.

Crowdfunding

Throughout history, people have been clubbing together to finance things. In the noughties, technology and terminology came together to spawn a new form of this: crowdfunding. It's something that has helped a number of Real Bread bakeries in our network to start up, re-equip or scale up.

How it works

You have an idea, plan how to make it a reality, work out how much it will cost and use this to set your target, then ask people to each pledge a portion of this target. Some crowdfunding platforms allow you to choose between receiving however much is pledged and an all-or-nothing campaign in which you only get the money if you reach your target. The latter is riskier but tends to raise more. Either way, you will pay the platform a fee and/or a percentage of the money raised.

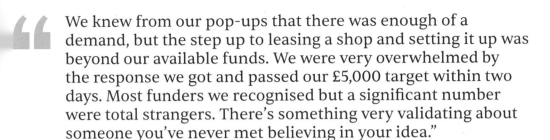

We knew from our pop-ups that there was enough of a demand, but the step up to leasing a shop and setting it up was beyond our available funds. We were very overwhelmed by the response we got and passed our £5,000 target within two days. Most funders we recognised but a significant number were total strangers. There's something very validating about someone you've never met believing in your idea."

Alex Tait, The Orange Bakery, Oxfordshire

Rewards

It's usual to offer incentives for people to support you, with larger rewards for larger pledges. Typical rewards from bakeries include pots of sourdough starter, a Real Bread subscription (eg a loaf a week for a given period of time), a place in a baking class or course, and bits of kit or clobber (dough scrapers, tote bags, T-shirts) perhaps branded with the bakery's logo. You might also want to throw a party for your backers if you reach your target.

We wrote up the names of all our backers in little oranges hanging from the branches of an enormous tree painted on the wall of our shop. We still get people walking in and pointing out theirs. We also had a party for about 200 who could come, where we served pizza and beer brewed from our old loaves."

Alex Tait, the Orange Bakery, Oxfordshire

Crowdfunding can also take the form of investments, the plan being that you repay backers (perhaps in the form of equity in the business) and maybe with interest. An example of a successful investment campaign is The Thoughtful Bakery in Bath raising £55,000 in 2012 to expand their bakehouse.

Tips

In 2015, Corinne Castle spoke to a number of Real Bread entrepreneurs for an article in our True Loaf magazine. Susan Clarke from Bread in Common in Staffordshire told her "Giving money isn't just about getting a perk but putting money into a social aim, building social capital." This was supported by Debbie Galton from The Good Loaf in Northampton, who works with female ex-offenders. "We also wanted to create buy-in from the local community and for people to feel involved in the café and bakery from the beginning."

Simon Cobb led a crowdfunding campaign that raised more than £23,000 in 2017 to fit out the not-for-profit social enterprise Stoneham Bakehouse in Hove, West Sussex. He said: "It seems silly to say this, but the crucial aspect of crowdfunding is the crowd. If you can build a group of people who like what you do and believe in your ethos, then you're a long way to success. Gathering a crowd can take time, so planning and promotion are crucial. We made a big effort from day one to use social and traditional media to let people know what we were doing, how they could get our bread, how to book classes, how to stay connected for updates. When it came to finding an actual bricks and mortar space, we asked our crowd for some help. When we launched the campaign, they were ready and waiting to make their pledges. Your crowdfunding backers can go on to become your customers and advocates. We're really thankful to those 273 people who enabled us to fit out our bakery and get baking, and everyone who has supported us since."

Simon's tips

- Build a crowd.
- Have a really well-defined offer (eg your money will pay for the oven, a mixer etc.)
- Give good rewards but be careful that their cost doesn't take a huge bite out of what you raise.
- A longer campaign doesn't necessarily mean more money. Ours lasted just two weeks. It was an intense period but meant that we didn't have the mid-campaign lull that can happen.

In 2020, Sophia Handschuh raised more than £32,000 in 28 days towards transforming Sourdough Sophia from a home-based microbakery into a high street business. She said: "I think what captured the crowd was the amount of buzz we created around the project. What helped the most, though, was being very clear about what we were going to do with the money."

Sophia's tips

- Set yourself a very clear goal, be transparent and make sure you constantly talk to your audience about this.
- Having a few key rewards to start with and adding new rewards at the halfway point is a very good way to get over that halfway lull, which inevitably does happen. Rather than panicking, make sure you are well prepared with further rewards.
- Writing to every possible newspaper, magazine and Instagram account that might mention you is what expands your crowd and makes the campaign successful.

Tech

A number of online platforms provide the tools for anyone to run a crowdfunding campaign relatively simply and cheaply. Each platform provides a wealth of video tutorials, blog posts and other guidance and will take a percentage, and perhaps a fee, from what you raise. Together with social media accounts, they enable you to spread the word and connect with potential backers beyond your existing network of family, neighbours, friends and professional contacts. You will still need to work hard and work smart, though. User-friendly video editing and graphic design platforms and downloadable software are also readily available, allowing even technophobes and people who feel their artistic skills are limited to make at least half-decent promotional media.

You can find out more about crowdfunding, and lists of platforms, from associations including:

- » www.ukcfa.org.uk
- » www.eurocrowd.org
- » www.cfinstitute.org

Going it alone

There are many benefits to using a crowdfunding platform that you might consider being worth the cut they take. You do, however, have the option of going it alone. Maggie Rich of Companions Real Bread CIC in Bedford said: "If you have a strong, existing supporter base in your local community and well-established lines of communication with them, it's possible to run a successful crowdfunding campaign without having to pay commission to a platform. We had a target of £5,000 and exceeded that by 25%. It was difficult to stop people giving!"

Grants and loans

Depending on who and whereabouts you are, and the size, type and stage of your business, you might be eligible for some form of financial support. Your government or local/regional authority might be able to offer or signpost you towards grants and loans, for example, as might your bank. See the next page for some places to look.

UK

- **The BEIS** runs this database: www.gov.uk/business-finance-support
- **Business Wales** provides and signposts a range of funding and other support. www.businesswales.gov.wales
- **My Funding Central** www.myfundingcentral.co.uk
- **Local Enterprise Partnerships** have Growth Hubs that can advise on funding and support. www.lepnetwork.net/growth-hubs
- **The Prince's Trust** works with people up to the age of 30. www.princes-trust.org.uk
- **Scottish Enterprise** provides and signposts a range of funding and other support. www.scottish-enterprise.com
- **Small Business** publishes a list of business grants. www.smallbusiness.co.uk
- **Start Up Loans** is a government-backed provider of low-interest loans, with free mentoring. www.startuploans.co.uk
- **UnLtd** provides mentoring and funding to social entrepreneurs. www.unltd.org.uk

A community owned/run bakery might be able to secure funding from The National Lottery Community Fund, Power to Change or the Community Ownership Fund.

Australia

Grants and assistance programmes in Australia can be found through the government's grant finder. The government also has an advisory service which can help new business owners find mentors.

- **Australian Government Grants and Programs Finder** www.business.gov.au/grants-and-programs
- **Small Business Finance** Created by the Australian Bankers' Association and CPA Australia to help small business investigate suitable finance options. www.financingyoursmallbusiness.com.au
- **Social Change** Central platform to help social entrepreneurs find funding and other support. www.socialchangecentral.com

Canada

The Canadian government offers a range of financial support options, including grants, loans, tax credits and wage subsidies. The government of each province also provides finance and guidance, on top of which there are private finance opportunities.

- **Government of Canada Business Benefits Finder**
  innovation.ised-isde.canada.ca
- **Mentor Works** A government programme to help you find and bid for funding.
  www.mentorworks.ca
- **Canada Startups** A site that can help you plan and find funding for your
  business idea. www.canadastartups.org
- **Innovation, Science and Economic Development Canada** Support and
  finance for social enterprises. www.ic.gc.ca/eic/site/053.nsf/eng/00009.html
- **Social Enterprise Council of Canada** Signposts places to find financial and
  other support. www.secouncil.ca

Ireland

- **Local Enterprise Office** Provides information, funding and other support.
  www.localenterprise.ie
- **Strategic Banking Corporation of Ireland** Run to make low-cost credit
  available to Irish SMEs. www.sbci.gov.ie
- **Rethink Ireland** Provides grants to social enterprises and charities for social
  innovations. www.rethinkireland.ie
- **Microfinance Ireland** Loans of up to €25,000 to start-up and existing micro
  enterprises. www.microfinanceireland.ie

New Zealand

There are few small business grants or loans available from the government. The
gateway to those on offer is the Regional Business Partner Network.

- **Regional Business Partner Network** www.regionalbusinesspartners.co.nz
- **Te Puni Kōkiri** Offers support to Māori business owners and start-up
  entrepreneurs. www.tpk.govt.nz
- **Social Enterprise Auckland** Provides a list of links to funders and other
  support. www.socialenterpriseauckland.org.nz/resources

Businesses can also apply to Companies Office for a Business Number (NZBN),
which can help owners to connect and interact through a shared information
network.

» www.nzbn.govt.nz

USA

Federal government offers little in the way of financial or other support to small business owners, so your best bet might be to investigate what your state or local authority provides. There are also many corporate and non-profit entities that offer small grants or awards. A number of government and private schemes are demographic-specific, aimed at supporting women entrepreneurs, people of First Nations, people from minority ethnic backgrounds, people in rural communities and people in economic disadvantage, for example.

- Grant Watch is a database for non-profits and small businesses. www.grantwatch.com
- Small Business Administration helps arrange and guarantee loans, and has a database of state/local organisations that offer various forms of support. www.sba.gov/funding-programs
- USAgov has links to information on financing your business. www.usa.gov/funding-options

I fought the law...

...and the law won. At times, doing things by the book might seem like a pain but make no mistake, it's nowhere near as painful as winging it and then getting caught out.

Although there are hoops to jump through when you make the leap from baking for yourself to baking for others, and yet more if your business gets larger and you become an employer, most regulations are based on fairness and common sense. As this is such a large topic (particularly in countries where regulations vary at the regional – and even more local – level) we have attempted to outline just some of the key areas for the UK, some general principles of which may be relevant elsewhere. We have also added a few basic notes for Australia, Canada, Ireland, New Zealand and the USA.

Another disclaimer

As with the rest of this book, while we have done our best to ensure accuracy of the information in this chapter, it is by no means exhaustive or definitive guidance/ advice, legal or otherwise. It is simply a starting point for your own independent research into the current rules and regs in your part of the world.

In the UK, the Food Standards Agency (FSA) operates in England, Northern Ireland and Wales, though its responsibilities differ between the nations. Food Standards Scotland (FSS) is responsible for the fourth nation in the union. Regulations are (currently) based on EU legislation and so are broadly similar, though there are some differences between the four nations. Following the UK's departure from the EU, most legislation was retained but may well be reviewed, added to, amended or revoked over time. In Northern Ireland, the majority of EU food hygiene and safety legislation will continue to apply, as per the Northern Ireland Protocol.

General

As the owner of a small food business anywhere in the world, key areas of law with which you need to comply will probably include:

- Business registration.
- Licensing.
- Food hygiene and safety.
- Inspection(s) before or when you start your business, and perhaps at intervals thereafter.
- Employment.
- Insurance.
- Tax.
- Weights and measures and other trading standards.
- Labelling and other consumer information.

There may well be others, for example regarding noise/nuisance, waste, ventilation and odour control, traffic/highways (eg for parking and access), data protection and privacy policy (eg customer records, mailing list), software licences, playing music etc. If anything changes about your business (eg size, turnover, what you do/sell, location, directors etc) be sure to look into whether different rules will apply. Get in touch with your local authority, or visit their website, to see what information and guidance they can provide or point you towards.

National governments also typically provide guidance on starting a food business. For example:

» **England, Northern Ireland, Wales** www.food.gov.uk/business-guidance/starting-a-food-business
» **Scotland** www.foodstandards.gov.scot/business-and-industry/advice-for-new-businesses
» **Australia** www.foodstandards.gov.au/foodsafety/standards/Pages/Home-based-food-businesses.aspx
» **Ireland** www.fsai.ie/food_businesses/starting_business/home_business_food_stall.html
» **New Zealand** www.mpi.govt.nz/food-business/starting-a-food-business/thinking-of-starting-a-new-food-business/
» **USA** www.fda.gov/food/food-industry/how-start-food-business

Registering your food business

Anyone starting a new food business of any size (so this includes home bakeries and CSBs) in the UK must register with the local authority (Shared Regulatory Services in Wales) at least 28 days before it starts trading. This applies if your business is operating for five or more days in any five consecutive weeks, so even if you only plan to bake once a week, if you do so every week then you will still need to register. You need to register all premises used for a food business, which includes market stalls and delivery vehicles.

The process is simple: you just need to fill out and return a registration form – some authorities offer online application. Registration cannot be refused and there is no charge. If you have more than one outlet for your loaves you may have to register them separately. If you use premises in more than one local authority area (eg your bakehouse is in one town and you own/rent a shop across the border in another authority's area), you must register with each authority separately. If you will be handling meat, fish, egg or dairy products you may require approval as well as registration.

Registering your business name

Sole traders and partnerships do not have to register a business name. For other legal forms of business, such as a limited company or limited partnership, registration is compulsory with Companies House. However, your product brand name and company name do not need to be the same.

Restrictions

There are certain names that cannot be used to prevent unfair trading. You may not use certain words or expressions in your business name, such as Royal, International, Authority, Group, Prince and Princess, European, Fund and Charity, unless you have proper entitlement.

Displaying your business name

Your business name, the name of the sole trader or partners' names and your business address should be printed on your stationery in accordance with the Companies Act 2006. This includes business letters, written orders for the supply of goods and services and invoices. It is an offence not to disclose your business details as requested.

Find out more:

» www.companieshouse.gov.uk/about/guidance.shtml

Planning permission

Unless using premises that are already in use as a bakery or similar, a new bakery will usually require planning permission for a change of use. Anyone can make an application, but you will need specialist information (your equipment supplier may be able to advise) to help ensure that your application is successful. Retrospective applications and non-compliance will end up costing you unnecessary time, money and aggravation.

Street trading

If you are planning to have a stall or market outdoors, then you may need to apply to your local authority for a street trading licence. If you are trading on private land (for example, on an area outside a community centre or church hall) then you may not need consent, but whoever owns the land may need planning permission. If you take a stall on a street market, the organiser will be able to advise you further.

Food safety and hygiene

These are of paramount importance to a food business, and the business owner is legally responsible for them. Failure to have and follow good food safety and hygiene procedures can result in being fined and/or having your business shut down, and you might even face legal action from an unwell customer.

Key basic principles

In the UK you must:

- Ensure food is safe to eat.
- Make sure food is of the nature, substance and quality you say it is.
- Not mislead people by the way you label or market (including how you advertise and present) food.
- Keep (and show when required) records of ingredients you use and food you buy to sell on.
- Withdraw unsafe food, complete an incident report and let people know (eg a poster or leaflet) why it has been withdrawn.

- Display your food hygiene (Food Hygiene Information Scheme in Scotland) rating, if in food service or retail.

The FSA suggests "the 4Cs" as a way of remembering the key processes to focus on to ensure good food hygiene: cleaning, cooking, chilling and cross-contamination.

Unless you are using meat or dairy products in your bakery, your local authority probably won't consider your business as high risk, but you still need to make a food hygiene plan to keep risks as low as possible. Some rules and processes are simple: making sure that no food, or anything containing food, ever touches the floor, for example. Ingredients and products should always go straight onto shelves, racks, pallets etc. Other steps that you might be advised or required to take can include installing two sinks - one for washing hands and another for equipment.

If you intend to use meat or dairy (mmm - cheesy bacon bread...) then you will need to take extra steps, which may include specific food safety training. Your local authority's environmental health or food safety officer (we've abbreviated both as EHO) might be able to provide some advice, though increasingly cash-strapped councils are tending to point people to private agencies/consultants for guidance.

- » www.food.gov.uk/business-guidance/general-food-law
- » www.food.gov.uk/business-guidance/food-hygiene-for-your-business

Hazard Analysis and Critical Control Point (HACCP)

This is how you manage the food hygiene and safety procedures of your business. It involves:

- Looking at your business, premises and processes and identifying potential risks - eg microbial, chemical or physical contamination.
- Focussing on any critical control points, steps in a process at which control can be applied to minimise/prevent a risk/hazard.
- Making a plan of procedures to follow to prevent/minimise the risks you have identified, and actions you will take when things go wrong.
- Monitoring to ensure your plan is being followed and working, and making revisions if it isn't.

The FSA has created the MyHACCP free web tool to help UK food businesses develop food safety management systems:

- » https://myhaccp.food.gov.uk

Cleaning

You should have routines for cleaning-as-you-go, end of shift, end of day, and even more thorough weekly and monthly deep cleans. Key areas are the ingredient storage space, production area, bins/waste disposal, mixer, oven and other equipment, toilets and (if applicable) service areas and staff room. This should all be done with appropriate detergents, disinfectants etc and all products that will be used on surfaces and equipment that will come into contact with food must be food-safe.

» www.food.gov.uk/business-guidance/cleaning-effectively-in-your-business

Personal hygiene

This is essential for all food handlers. Your procedures and practice should include:

- Frequent, thorough hand washing and drying, including but not limited to before handling food, between tasks and after all breaks, nose blowing and phone handling (eg to Instagram your latest creation).
- Calling in sick following a bout of vomiting or diarrhoea and not returning to work until 48 hours after symptoms stop.
- Keeping long hair tied back or, better still, covered by a net.
- Not eating, smoking, chewing gum or touching the face in a food storage, production or service area.
- Only ever coughing or sneezing into the crook of the elbow and never over food, storage, production or service areas.
- Wearing an apron or other clean protective clothing.
- Storing personal clothes and other items away from storage, production and service areas.
- Keeping fingernails short and not wearing nail polish, which can flake off.
- Not wearing jewellery, or only wearing plain-banded rings and sleeper earrings.
- Covering any cut or wound with a waterproof blue plaster, which can be spotted more easily if it comes off. If on the hand, wear a disposable glove over the top.
  » www.food.gov.uk/business-guidance/personal-hygiene

Food hygiene training

A food handler is anyone involved in a food business who handles or prepares food whether open (unwrapped) or packaged. The operator of a food business should ensure that all food handlers are made aware of the importance of, are trained (or at least instructed) in and supervised in following good food hygiene practices. The level and type of training needed will depend on the tasks a food handler carries out and types of food involved.

It is important that anyone who is handling food is aware of the essentials of food hygiene. It's not a legal requirement for all food handlers to have attended a training course on food hygiene, though you may want to offer this, especially if you employ more than a few people. If your EHO considers your business to be 'high risk', staff might need to receive more detailed training. Further training for managers might also be required.

> » www.food.gov.uk/foodindustry/regulation/hygleg/hyglegresources/sfbb/sfbbcaterers/
> » www.food.gov.uk/foodindustry/regulation/hygleg/hygleginfo/foodhygknow/

Inspection

Once you have registered as a food business, an EHO from the local council may visit your premises to carry out an inspection – in Scotland it is a requirement. Don't feel intimidated by this – most microbakers report that their EHO was very friendly and informative in helping them to ensure that they met the grade. Microbaker Devika Tamang, for example, said: "The man from the council came and conducted an inspection of my kitchen, which is where I will be baking. It was a useful, informative and enjoyable experience for me. I am more confident now that I have had the inspection and know what the inspector is looking for and how they can help me comply with legal requirements."

Things that the EHO will be looking out for include that

- Your premises are clean and maintained in good condition.
- There is adequate lighting and ventilation.
- All food preparation equipment is clean, in good condition and easily kept hygienic. Some EHOs may argue that wood is not an appropriate material for food preparation (see below) or that second-hand equipment is not hygienic.
- You have enough workspace to carry out tasks hygienically.
- You have appropriate facilities to protect your food from pests (and pets).
- Food is stored at appropriate temperatures – this particularly applies to meat and dairy products. The EHO may check that you have reduced the risk of cross-contamination in a fridge – eg sealable storage containers, raw meat stored below all other foods and no leaks or spills.
- Staff members (even if that's just you) have access to a toilet (or toilets, depending on the number of employees), which must not open directly into rooms where you handle food.

- A washbasin just for cleaning hands (ie not for washing equipment or any activity that involves food) has been installed in the food preparation area.
- Disinfectants and other cleaning chemicals are not stored in areas where food is handled.
- Any vehicle you use to transport foods is also kept clean and maintained in good condition.
- Items used to hold food (eg boxes and trays) in vehicles must not be used for transporting anything other than foods where this may cause contamination. If you do transport anything other than foods, you must keep the items separate so that there is no risk of food becoming contaminated.

If you are using domestic spaces for your food business, you will need to demonstrate that you are taking steps to ensure that this dual use will not compromise safety and hygiene – eg it is good practice to (and your EHO may insist that you) have separate food preparation equipment for the bakery and your own domestic use.

Interpretation

While there are hard and fast rules, much is left to the opinion of and interpretation by local authorities and even individual EHOs. For example, several local authorities insist on their websites that wooden work surfaces aren't suitable in food preparation areas, stating the source of this is EU legislation. The actual wording of Annex II, Chapter II, Para. 1(f) of Regulation (EC) No 852/2004 on the hygiene of foodstuffs is: "surfaces (including surfaces of equipment) in areas where foods are handled and in particular those in contact with food are to be maintained in a sound condition and be easy to clean and, where necessary, to disinfect. This will require the use of smooth, washable, corrosion-resistant and non-toxic materials, unless food business operators can satisfy the competent authority that other materials used are appropriate." We haven't been able to find specific mention, let alone prohibition, of 'wood' or 'wooden' in any relevant national legislation or FSA guidance.

Other things we have heard of EHOs expressing hygiene or health and safety concerns about are the use of a wood-fired oven (someone or something's gonna BURN!) and a sourdough starter. (Bacteria? Arggh!)* Again, we've been unable to find legislative prohibition of, or national guidance against using, either of these.

Having read the relevant legislation, if there is something that your EHO insists you can or cannot do, which goes against your understanding of it, you could try asking them (politely) to point you to the specific section and to talk you through it. If what they say still doesn't seem right, try asking for a second opinion or for the matter to be escalated internally for review. If this doesn't work out, taking the matter further is a challenge. Referral/arbitration isn't a service advertised by either The Chartered Trading Standards Institute or the Chartered Institute of Environmental Health. You could try Citizens Advice or the Food Standards Agency, but we don't know how far you'll get.

*In both cases we're paraphrasing, of course, but that was the gist of what bakers have reported to us.

Acrylamide

First detected in food in 2002, acrylamide is a substance formed from the amino acid asparagine and sugars naturally present in certain foods when they are cooked at temperatures higher than 120°C in low moisture conditions. Examples include baked or fried carbohydrate-rich foods, such as bread and other baked goods; crisps and chips; and coffee.

Acrylamide has been declared a carcinogenic substance by the European Food Standards Agency. Regulation (EU) 2017/2158 establishing mitigation measures and benchmark levels for the reduction of acrylamide in food came into force in April 2018. At the time of writing, the possibility of maximum permitted levels is still under discussion and official guidance for both SME bakers and local authority enforcement agents in the UK is limited. It seems likely that requirements and enforcement will be refined and tightened over time, though.

As an SME bakery food business operator (FBO) you are expected to:

- Be aware of acrylamide as a food safety hazard and have a general understanding of how acrylamide is formed in baked goods.
- Take the necessary steps to mitigate acrylamide formation, adopting relevant measures as part of your food safety management procedures.
- Keep records of the mitigation measures you have undertaken.

Methods of mitigation outlined in the Food and Drink Europe Acrylamide Toolbox are:

- Choosing ingredients/cereal varieties with naturally low asparagine levels, grown in ways that do not elevate them.[1]
- Reducing proportion of bran/wholegrain ingredients.[2]
- Replacing some wheat flour with flour lower in asparagine, eg rice.
- Avoiding ammonium bicarbonate as a raising agent.[3]

- Increasing piece size/volume to surface ratio.
- Prolonging fermentation time.
- Lowering pH/adding organic acids – sourdough fermentation does this!
- Baking for shorter times and/or at lower temperatures.[4]

Notes

1. Sulphur deprivation, excessive use of nitrogen fertiliser and fungal infection have all been found to increase asparagine levels. There are questions hanging over GM crops being developed to have lower levels.
2. Asparagine is concentrated in the germ and bran. The toolbox acknowledges the problem is that this will 'significantly compromise the product's organoleptic and nutritional properties.'
3. Chemical leavening is not an issue for Real Bread but is used in some cakes, soda loaves, biscuits etc.
4. While not an accurate measure, darker browning is an indicator that a product will have higher acrylamide levels.

FBOs are also expected to arrange for sampling and analysis 'where appropriate' to monitor acrylamide levels as part of their assessment of the mitigation measures, and to keep records of sampling plans and results of any testing.

NB The Food Standards Agency's guidance for local authorities states that "Some level of flexibility and discretion may be required in terms of what is expected of small and micro-businesses. Account should be taken of what is reasonable and proportionate to a specific FBO's situation and resources." How and to what extent you adhere to the regulations and guidelines is another case of interpretation and any dispute with an EHO would be a case of arguing your interpretation against theirs and, if that doesn't work, escalating the matter – see pages 108 to 109.

Find out more:
  » www.food.gov.uk/business-guidance/acrylamide-legislation
  » https://eur-lex.europa.eu/legal-content/EN/TXT/?uri=CELEX:32017R2158
  » https://ec.europa.eu/food/safety/chemical_safety/contaminants/catalogue/acrylamide_en

Bread weights

It is legal to sell loaves of any weight in the UK.

- Prepacked/wrapped: the weight must be shown clearly in grams on the wrapper or label.

- Unwrapped/loose, and pre-packed for direct sale (PPDS): you must display the weight for each product at point of sale, either on the packaging or some form of ticket, label or signage that the customer can see easily.*

Unwrapped loaves/buns that weigh 400g or multiples of 400g (eg 800g), or under 300g, are exempt. For the sake of transparency, however, we urge all bakers and retailers to display the weight of all loaves.

The other exemption is in the case of a wholesale contract for loaves weighing a total of 25kg or more in each delivery, which will be weighed on delivery, and eaten on the premises (eg restaurant or café) of the buyer.

In May 2021, the Office for Product Safety and Standards in England advised us that if you cut large loaves into pieces (eg halves or quarters) you must weigh each piece and show the weight in grams on the label (if prepacked) or advise the customer of the weight of each, either using point of sale labels/signage or verbally (if unpackaged or PPDS).

*Pre-packed for direct sale (PPDS) means food made, sealed (including by a sticker, band or tag) in a bag/wrapper/container *before* the customer orders it and then sold from the same premises. It also includes food sold by the business at a different location, such as a farmers' market stall run by its employees.

Average weights

In medieval times, bakers in London who sold underweight loaves could be dragged through the city's streets on a hurdle. That penalty is long gone but you can still be fined or even imprisoned. In the UK, the average system of quantity control applies to all loaves (packaged and unpackaged) weighing more than 5g but less than 25kg. The three requirements that need to be met are:

- The *average* weight of loaves in a batch* at the time of purchase mustn't be less than the nominal weight (NW) ie the one you state on the label/signage.
- No more than 1 in 40 loaves in the batch may weigh less than the NW minus the tolerable negative error (TNE – see below).
- None of the loaves in the batch may weigh less than NW – (2 x TNE)

*Calculate this by dividing the total weight of all loaves in the batch by the number of loaves in the batch.

The TNE depends on the nominal weight:

Nominal weight	Tolerable negative error
300g to 500g	3% of the nominal weight
500g to 1,000g	15g
1,000g to 10,000g	1.5% of the nominal weight

For loaves marketed as 400g/800g this means:

1. The mean average weight of loaves in a batch can't be less than 400g/800g
2. No more than 1 in 40 loaves in a batch can weigh less than 388g/785g
3. No baked loaf can weigh less than 376g/770g

In May 2021, the Office for Product Safety and Standards in England advised us that, as this average weight system is more appropriate for larger bakeries and packers, smaller bakeries should instead weigh each piece to ensure that it is at least the weight stated.

As bread loses weight through evaporation during and after cooling, it is advisable to do your checks *after* cooling. If you need to weigh bread while still hot, for each product you will need to go through a process of determining average weight loss between the end of baking and the last time on which it is available for sale. You can then work out how much each must weigh when hot to comply with all three rules when sold.

The scales you use must have divisions of no more than 2g. They must also be marked CE or UKCA and stickered with the letter M as fit for trade use, or (if older) crown stamped.

If you pre-pack loaves, you must keep written records of your weight checks and it is advised that you do so for loose loaves as well.

Find out more at:
  » www.businesscompanion.info/en/quick-guides/weights-and-measures/small-bakers-and-average-weight
  » www.nibusinessinfo.co.uk/content/weights-and-measures-rules-bakers

Labelling

In the UK, what you are required to declare and how you must do so depends on whether the food is sold:

- **Non-prepacked:** sold loose or packed after the customer has selected/ordered it – eg a loaf dropped in a bag after being chosen from a display, or a sandwich made to order.
- **Pre-packed for direct sale (PPDS):** packed before the customer selects/orders it but on the site where it was made – eg a bakery, or at a site operated by the producer such as a farmers' market stall run by the bakery or retail outlet supplied from the bakery's central production unit.
- **Pre-packed:** sealed packaging before the customer orders/selects it and sold by a third party – eg bagged up to be sold by a local retailer.

Non-prepacked

All that you are legally required to declare are the:

- Name of the food (eg wholemeal bread).
- Full ingredients list.
- The presence of allergens (see below).
- Quantitative ingredients declaration (QUID) on any product containing meat.

We urge all bakers/retailers to display this information clearly at the point of sale (eg shelf tickets or prominent signage) and/or on labels applied to any bag/packaging used after product selection, and we continue lobbying the government to make this mandatory. If you choose the label option, you will need to follow the rules for PPDS food.

You are, however, legally permitted to give this information verbally, in which case you must display a notice inviting customers to ask for it.

If you sell food online or by phone or mail order, customers must be able to get this information for free before they buy. You must provide the information on your website, in your catalogue or set up a freephone number for them to call.

Pre-packed for direct sale

Following years of campaigning by organisations including The Allergy Alliance, the Real Bread Campaign and, notably, the family of Natasha Ednan-Laperouse, rather than being able to give the above information verbally for PPDS food, you now must declare it on a label.

The way you do so must be in line with the food law requirements that apply in your nation – see link below. If you have used fortified flour (which in the UK is most flour except wholemeal) you need to declare the so-called fortificants, as listed by the miller eg: wheat flour [wheat flour, calcium carbonate, iron, niacin, thiamine].

If you choose to declare more information than legally required, you need to follow the guidelines for pre-packed food in full – ie you can't pick and choose.

Pre-packed

You must display the following mandatory information on the product packaging or on a label attached to the packaging:

- The name of the food.
- The quantitative ingredients declaration (QUID) if and as needed.
- A list of ingredients, emphasising any allergens.
- The net weight of the food.
- A best before or use by date.
- Your business name and address.

The way you do so must be in line with the food law requirements that apply in your nation.

Allergen notification

There are many things to which some people have allergies, but the 14 that you must declare by law are: celery, cereals containing gluten (wheat, rye, barley, oats, triticale), crustaceans (prawns, crabs and lobsters etc), eggs, fish, lupin (aka lupine), milk, molluscs (eg mussels and oysters), mustard, peanuts, sesame, soybeans, sulphur dioxide and sulphites (if at more than 10ppm) and tree nuts (almonds, Brazil nuts, cashews, hazelnuts, walnuts, pecans, pistachios and macadamia etc).

The presence of an allergen from this list in an ingredient you use might not be immediately obvious. For example, fish sauce might be made from crustaceans, while both gluten and soy find their way into all sorts of things. Always read the label.

You must:

- Ensure that you and any employees receive allergen training, which can be done online through the Food Standards Agency (FSA).
- Handle and manage allergens in accordance with official guidance, segregating them to avoid cross-contamination if at all possible.

- Keep written records of allergens you use, for example in product information sheets.
- Notify customers of their presence.

The basics for allergen notification are:

- **Prepacked food:** must have a full ingredients list on the packaging and allergens must be emphasised (eg in bold) each time they appear on this list.
- **Food pre-packed for direct sale (PPDS):** as for prepacked food.
- **Non-prepacked/loose food:** notification of allergens can be done verbally by staff or on a menu/sign/poster/chalkboard etc. Alternatively, you can display a statement advising customers that one or more of the 14 allergens has been used, plus clear direction of how they can find out the details from you – eg ask a staff member, see poster by the till. Though you don't have to give a full ingredients list, we strongly encourage you to do so.
- **Delivery and distance selling:** you must provide allergen information both before the customer purchases the food (eg on your website for online sales, or verbally for phone orders) and when it is delivered (eg labels on the food/ packaging, or a menu/information sheet). Allergen information should also be available to a customer in written form at a point between a customer placing the order and taking delivery of it.

Note on free-from claims

The FSA notes that: "Making free-from claims for foods requires strict controls of ingredients, how they are handled and how they are prepared. A free-from claim is a guarantee that the food is suitable for all with an allergy or intolerance. For example, if you are handling wheat flour in a kitchen and you cannot remove the risk of cross-contamination through segregation by time and space, you should let the customer know. You should not make any gluten-free or wheat-free claims."

Note on 'ancient' wheats

Spelt (*T. spelta* or *T. aestivum spelta*), einkorn (*T. monococcum*), emmer (*T. turgidum dicoccum also called farro*), khorasan (*T. turgidum turanicum*, trademarked as Kamut) and durum (*T. turgidum durum*) are all types of wheat. Although they differ from modern/common/bread wheat (*Triticum aestivum*) and some people who struggle with common wheat might be able to enjoy eating bread made with one or more of these 'ancient' wheats, they cannot be marketed as 'wheat free' and must be emphasised on ingredients lists according to allergen regulations. Also see the notes on health and nutrition claims on page 118.

Find out more:
  » Food Labelling Regulations 1996 (as amended)
    www.opsi.gov.uk/si/si1996/Uksi_19961499_en_1.htm
  » www.gov.uk/guidance/food-labelling-giving-food-information-to-consumers
  » www.food.gov.uk/business-guidance/labelling-guidance-for-prepacked-for-
    direct-sale-ppds-food-products
  » www.gov.uk/guidance/food-labelling-loose-foods
  » www.food.gov.uk/business-guidance/allergen-guidance-for-food-businesses
  » www.sustainweb.org/realbread/bakers_support/
  » www.sustainweb.org/realbread/bread_labelling/
  » www.sustainweb.org/realbread/real_bread_loaf_mark

Optional information

Having met mandatory labelling requirements, you might choose to provide
additional information, such as:

  • Your bakery logo – build that brand awareness!
  • A one-line description, if it will add genuine and useful information – eg
    hand-crafted from Kent Old Hoary flour produced by Windy Miller, fermented
    overnight and baked in a wood-fired oven.
  • The Real Bread Loaf Mark, if you have signed up to the scheme.
  • Bakery website.
  • Social media handles/hashtags, if you're into that kind of thing.

If you have space, you might also add a note along the lines of: "Store in a cool, dry
place (such as a bread bin) or slice and freeze. Do not store in the fridge as this can
speed staling and encourage mould growth."

Legal (and honest) marketing

As we outline in the Marketing chapter, there are so many positive things that you
can say about your locally produced Real Bread to help it sell like hot cakes. The
description and any claim that you use in marketing your loaves, however, must be
true and must not mislead your customers as to the true nature of the product. This
is not only a request from the Real Bread Campaign (after all, we put a lot of effort
into keeping an eye on the big players falling short in these respects), it's also the law

A guiding principle is that you should be honest and trustworthy and have evidence to back up your claims. For example:

- By law, the word 'organic' can only be used by a business that has been inspected and certified by an authorised body. If your business is not certified, you could not advertise your bread as 'made with organic flour', for example.
- The Bread and Flour Regulations (1998) state that you can only use the word 'wholemeal' in the name (eg 'wholemeal and white') or marketing (eg 'contains wholemeal goodness') of a wheat loaf if all of the flour used is wholemeal. Otherwise, the word wholemeal is only allowed to appear in the ingredients list.
- Similarly, you can only use 'wheat germ' as a descriptor if you have added prepared wheat germ to account for at least 10% of the weight of the dry ingredients.
- You should not use 'yeast free' or similar in the description of sourdough loaves. The natural leaven in sourdough contains one or more types of yeast, maybe even including Saccharomyces cerevisiae, the same species (though perhaps a different strain) as commercial bakers' and brewers' yeast. An alternative could be 'no added bakers' yeast'.
- In the UK and elsewhere there are laws regulating claims regarding gluten – gluten-free, low gluten etc.

If in any doubt, contact your local authority's trading standards department/officer. Incidentally, the commonly used word 'Granary' is a registered trademark of H*vis. We see it used for all sorts of brown and bitty loaves but legally it can only be used in accordance with rules laid down by the trademark holder. Possible alternatives include malthouse and malted.

An honest crust

We are calling for a change in law to make the following legal requirements and encourage all bakers and retailers to follow them in the meantime:

- The word 'sourdough' should only be used if the product is made without additives and leavened using a live starter culture and no other raising agent.
- 'Wholegrain' should only be used if at least 51% by weight of the dry ingredients are unrefined grains.
- 'Fresh', 'freshly baked', 'baked today' and other claims of freshness should only be used if the product has been made from scratch in the past 24 hours. Can't be used for 'bake off' products.

- Descriptors such as 'traditional', 'heritage', 'artisan', 'craft', 'farmhouse', 'ancient grains' should only be used appropriately – eg a loaf made using 5% spelt flour should not be marketed using the terms 'heritage' or 'ancient grains', and it would be disingenuous to market a factory loaf using any of the other descriptors.

Health and nutrition claims

Given the growing body of evidence (perhaps including positive personal experiences that you or customers have had) it is understandable that you might feel justified in saying your sourdough bread is 'more digestible' or 'gut friendly'. You might even feel you have good reason to say that it is safe for someone with coeliac disease (or who has some other medical reason for eliminating wheat or gluten from their diet) to eat sourdough. You might have similar urges regarding heritage or ancient grains. It is not legal to do any of this.

In the EU, the use of health and nutrition claims is controlled by Regulation (EC) No 1924/2006 and all that are permitted are listed in the EU Register of Nutrition and Health Claims. None of these relates to sourdough or different types of wheat. The UK implementation of this Regulation survived the Brexit transition and (at the time of writing) official governmental guidance is still available as is The Committee of Advertising Practice's advice on making health claims in non-broadcast advertising.

We continue to call for investment into research that will help to prove – or disprove – our beliefs around the potential benefits of sourdough and heritage wheats so that we can be sure which can be presented as facts. In the meantime, please stay within this law and, unless you are a registered physician with the qualification, expertise and licence to practise in the relevant field, don't give out medical advice, or anything that could be construed as such.

Find out more:
» www.gov.uk/government/publications/nutrition-and-health-claims-guidance-to-compliance-with-regulation-ec-1924-2006-on-nutrition-and-health-claims-made-on-foods

Australia and New Zealand

The standards and requirements are broadly the same in the two countries, though some differences exist. Key steps to opening a food business are:

- Find out if you need to register your food business (almost certainly yes).
- Determine your business classification.
- Check what permits/licences you might need and apply for them.
- Register the business with your local authority.
- Check and comply with food safety and hygiene requirements.

Further considerations in Australia

- Each Australian state and territory classifies food businesses differently.
- If you plan to build or renovate a building, check with your council about registration before you start.
- Is a food business permitted in the planning zone in which you intend to operate?
- All employees who handle food must be trained in food safety.
- No matter the size of your operation, or how often you sell food, a home-based food business is subject to the same food safety requirements as other food businesses.
- In NSW, VIC, QLD and ACT having a nominated food safety supervisor, who must be trained and certified, is mandatory.
- You'll need to tell your local council before changing your business name, location or activities.
- There may be limits on size, number and location of any business signage.
- In the case of residential premises, there may be a limit on the number of non-residents who can be employed there.
- The Australian Business Licence and Information Service (ABLIS) has a useful online tool to help you find the licences and information you need to start, run and grow your business: https://ablis.business.gov.au/.

Registration in New Zealand

Under the Food Act 2014, you will need to follow a food control plan, or National Programme for making and selling food. Lower and medium-risk businesses follow a National Programme. This means they don't need to use written Food Control Plans, but must register the business, meet food safety standards, keep some records, and get checked. Bread making is covered by the MPI generic National Programme 2 (NP2). As a NP2 business you can be verified by either the MPI or a verification officer from the local authority where the business is registered.

An NP2 business needs to be verified every three years and registration needs to be renewed with the local authority every two years.

» www.mpi.govt.nz/dmsdocument/21850-National-Programme-2-Guidance

Food safety and hygiene

To ensure you meet your legal obligations, the following are some of the key things to consider doing. Depending on your state or territory, some of these may be mandatory.

- Read the Australia New Zealand Food Standards Code.
- Determine who is responsible for the food safety of your business.
- Check who needs to have food safety training.
- Hire a trained and certified food safety supervisor and check if one needs to be on staff and available at all times.
- Work with your food safety supervisor to create and implement a food safety programme, which your local council will check to ensure it meets food laws and regulations.

Find out more:
- » www.foodsafety.com.au/blog/how-do-i-start-a-food-business
- » www.mpi.govt.nz/food-business/starting-a-food-business/thinking-of-starting-a-new-food-business/

Labelling

Pre-packed food must be labelled with information including:

- Name of the food.
- List of ingredients, in descending order by weight.
- Name and address of the supplier.
- Advisory statements, warning statements and declarations (eg regarding notifiable allergens).
- Best before (or, in the case of bread, baked on) date, plus use by date if required.
- Storage conditions and directions for use, if applicable.
- Nutrition information.
- Information about characterising ingredients (eg the % by weight of walnuts in a walnut loaf).
- Product weight (see below).

Food that is sold loose/unpackaged, is made and packaged on the premises from which it is sold, or packed in the presence of the customer, does not have to be labelled. Certain information (including notifiable allergens) however, must be made available to the customer by signage accompanying the food or displayed in connection with it, or upon request.

Find out more:
  » www.foodstandards.gov.au/consumer/labelling
  » www.foodstandards.gov.au/code
  » www.mpi.govt.nz/food-business/labelling-composition-food-drinks/

Bread weights

Pre-packed bread and packs of biscuits/cookies must be sold by weight and you must show on the label the product net weight, in grams, at time of sale. Unless you package and sell the product on the same site, you must also include the name and street address of the production site. Some items can be sold by item count, rather than weight. They include single-serve bread rolls, croissants, buns, biscuits/cookies, pikelets, muffins, doughnuts and bagels. If you choose (as the Real Bread Campaign suggests) voluntarily to display the weight of unwrapped bread, or pre-packed products sold by item count, you must use approved scales and follow guidelines. Full requirements can be found on the DISER website.

  » www.industry.gov.au/regulations-and-standards/selling-bread-and-bakery-products

Canada

You will need to check and follow federal, provincial and municipal legislation. Some regulations differ between the country's 13 territories and provinces. Generally, you will need to:

- Register the business name.
- Apply for a municipal business licence.
- Check zoning regulations permit your type of business where you want to run it.
- Secure a business number (BN).
- Register your business with your province, and other governing bodies if required locally.
- Register for the GST/HST and PST, if applicable (see page 83).
- Check your legal liabilities and insurance requirements.

- Check differences in legislation if you will sell food in another province.
- Follow labelling and composition requirements.
- Follow food safety laws.
- Check if you need Food Handler Certification.
- Arrange an inspection, if required.

Bread of any weight can be sold. Most foods that are pre-packed for sale must be labelled in full, which includes net weight in grams. Bread sold loose is exempt from these labelling regulations.

The Canadian Institute of Food Safety provides start-up business guidance and food safety law by location:

» www.foodsafety.ca/laws-requirements
» https://resources.foodsafety.ca/topic/opening-food-business

Find out more:

» https://inspection.canada.ca/food-label-requirements/eng/1574436698583/1574436791492
» https://inspection.canada.ca/food-label-requirements/labelling/industry/grain-and-bakery-products/eng/1392135900214/1392135960867?chap=2#s7c2

Ireland

As regulations in the Republic of Ireland are based on EU legislation, they are broadly similar to those in the UK – see above. For example, you will need to:

- Register your business with a competent authority (probably the local environmental health office).
- Familiarise yourself with, and follow, food hygiene legislation.
- Implement an HACCP food safety management system.
- Keep records of food businesses that supply you and that you supply.
- Arrange food safety training and supervision for food handlers.
- Provide food information to consumers that is accurate, clear, easy to understand and not misleading.

Labelling requirements are also more or less the same as in the UK, though the only information you are required to provide for unwrapped loaves/food is an allergen declaration. You can (and we encourage you to) provide other information voluntarily, which you would have to do in accordance with the FIC regulations.

Find out more:

> » www.fsai.ie/food_businesses/starting_business.html
> » www.fsai.ie/food_businesses/starting_business/home_business_food_stall.html
> » www.fsai.ie/legislation/food_legislation/food_information_fic/general_fic_provisions.html

USA

Your food business will be subject to Food and Drug Administration (FDA) and other federal, state and local requirements. You will need to check what these are and follow them. In general you must:

- Decide on your business type (see pages 44 and 45) and register it.
- Get a city or state business licence.
- Get a food service licence or permit, if applicable.
- Register your food facility with the FDA (a private residence is exempt from this).
- Check the Cottage Food Law in your state (see page 47) for food labelling requirements etc.
- Find out if you need a Reseller's Permit.
- Check if there are other state, county or city licences and permits you need.
- Obtain a food safety certification.
- Arrange a site inspection.
- Keep written, 'one up, one down' supply chain records: this means details of ingredients you buy and the source/supplier of each, as well as of your wholesale customers, and of packagers, if you use any.

Baked products of any weight can be sold. According to federal regulations, if a product weighs up to ½ pound it is legally defined as a roll or bun and over this weight it is bread.

Find out more:

> » www.fda.gov/food/food-industry/how-start-food-business

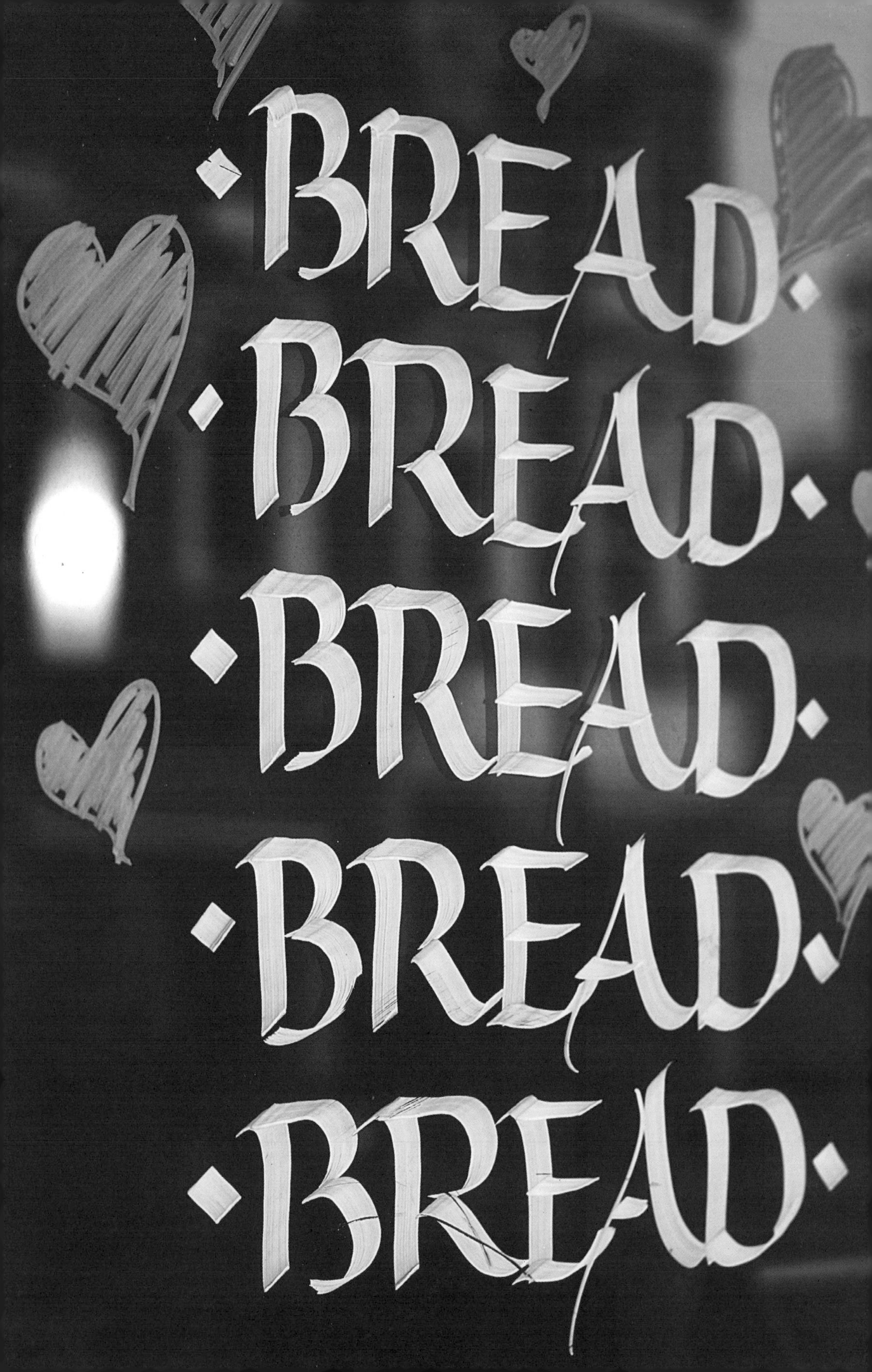
·BREAD·
·BREAD·
·BREAD·
·BREAD·
·BREAD·

Marketing

You're baking the best Real Bread that you can bake, right? Selling honest loaves at an honest price? You've gone to great lengths to ensure that each loaf looks, smells and – most importantly – tastes fantastic? Great, because Real Bread is what it's all about. Now, where are those customers? This is where marketing comes in.

Back in 2010, The Handmade Bakery co-founder Dan McTiernan told us: "Our main key is to adhere to [marketing guru] Seth Godin's mantra of being a 'purple cow'. By this he means be remarkable. We try to keep pushing what we do and how we do it both to keep up our own ethical and political aims of trying to change our community's connection with food for the better, and because we recognise that only by thinking creatively and building on what we have done before will we be satisfied. By doing these things we have attracted the attention of regional and national press, radio and television."

What is marketing?

Marketing is more than just advertising. It is "the homework that managers undertake to assess needs, measure their extent and intensity and determine whether a profitable opportunity exists. Marketing continues throughout the product's life, trying to find new customers by improving product appeal and performance, learning from product sales results and managing repeat performance." Philip Kotler et al, *Principles of Marketing*, Pearson Education, 2002

Successful marketing can be summed up in five Ps:

- The right Product.
- For the right Person.
- In the right Place.
- At the right Price.
- With the right Promotion.

Two sides of the story

Elements of the marketing mix need to be considered from the perspective of both the owner of the bakery and its customers:

Baker	Customer
What do you want to make and sell?	What do people want to buy?
Who do you want as customers?	Who is interested in being your customer?
Where do you want to be based?	Where do your potential customers live?
How much do you need and want to charge?	How much are customers able and prepared to pay?
What messages do you want and need to convey and how do you want to communicate them?	What information, story and imagery will help convince people to buy what you sell at the price you charge?

Successful marketing involves finding ways of maximising the overlap between answers in the two columns.

Marketing ingredients

Marketing can involve many different processes. The ones that we will look at here are:

- Market research.
- Differentiation.
- Promotion.
- Public relations.

We'll cover media relations in the next chapter.

Market research

The 'market' is the collective term for your potential customers; the 'research' bit is finding out who and where they are and what they want. There are various ways of doing this, including:

- Sampling: giving out tasters of breads you are considering making and asking which customers prefer and would buy and how much they'd be prepared to pay.
- A questionnaire: what people buy, when, what for etc (see below).
- Food mapping: looking at where people can already buy loaves (Real Bread and otherwise) locally and the prices charged.
- The Real Bread Map can be used in conjunction with local research to find an area without a place to buy Real Bread.

If your business plan relies on being located in a neighbourhood where people have a higher average income, sources of data might be available to help you identify one. For example, the Office of National Statistics publishes income estimates for 'Middle layer Super Output Areas' of 5,000 to 15,000 households in England and Wales.

  » www.ons.gov.uk

Questionnaires

Things you might ask in a questionnaire include:

- What type(s) of loaf do you usually buy? (eg white sandwich loaf?)
- How many loaves a week?
- From where? (eg supermarket, farmers' market stall, small bakery...)
- If you had the choice would you buy a different type? (eg wholemeal, sourdough)
- What day(s) are you most likely to buy bread?
- What time of day? (morning, afternoon, early evening)
- How much do you think is a fair price for a large/small loaf?
- Would you be prepared to pay a little more for a loaf if you knew it was crafted without additives by a local employer?
- Anything else that might help convince you to buy?
- What might make you less likely to buy from a small bakery? (eg price, opening hours, distance, choice)

Try to resist the temptation (with which this book's author struggles) to ask everything you want to know. The more questions you ask, the fewer people will complete the survey.

> How you word your questions is very important. For example, if you just ask people how much they would like to pay for a loaf, the answer may not be very much! Asking 'How much are you willing to pay for a medium-sized, additive-free loaf, made slowly by hand using local ingredients?' and then giving a range of price options may elicit a more useful response."
>
> *Ian Waterland, Knead Good Bread, Leicestershire*

Be careful what conclusions you draw from the responses. As with any survey, the results will be skewed by the people who can be bothered taking it. They might not necessarily reflect the local market accurately – eg the 80% of respondents who say they love your bread and are happy to pay whatever you need to charge might be 100% of the only 20 people in your neighbourhood who will actually do so.

Your elevator pitch

How do you sum up your business – and what sets it apart from your competitors – concisely and memorably in one or two short lines? This is useful to have up your sleeve ready for anyone to whom you need to 'sell' your business, be that a funder, journalist or potential customer at a farmers' market stall.

What's in a name?

A good business name should set you apart from your competitors and reflect the image you wish to project. It might also clarify the types of products you sell, your production methods or company values. The name can embody or imply one or more of the factors you believe to be fundamental to your business's identity. Is your bakery traditional, trustworthy, wholesome, rustic, cool, cutting-edge, a disruptor, wacky, urban, fun, inclusive, affordable, luxurious? Could your location (eg village name) or element(s) of local heritage be reflected in the name? Should your name be involved? Similar considerations apply to naming new products.

You can do worse than picking something simple that's easy to spell, pronounce and remember. This will make things easier for suppliers, potential customers and getting your name known. It's also worthwhile choosing a unique moniker that's available as a domain name and social media handle.

Logo-a-go-go

This is a key part of your brand identity. It should grab people's attention, then be memorable and become linked in their minds to what you do and how you do it, triggering positive feelings that will help to build brand loyalty. In combination with your business name, how your shop looks and other visual cues, people will infer from it the sort of business it is – perhaps your ethos, values and price point – before even setting foot inside your shop or approaching your stall or website. It will help potential customers to decide whether your business is 'for them'. It's something that you might decide is worth paying a specialist agency/designer to create for you. Then again, a naive doodle might nail it.

Packaging

The design of, and on, your packaging is another element of your brand identity. This even extends to what it's made from – the medium is the message, as media theorist Marshall McLuhan said. Recycled, biodegradable, brown kraft paper bag 'reads' very differently than a thin blue plastic carrier, or a hand-folded (and perhaps tied) sheet of waxed paper. Whatever you choose, it needs to be food-safe (check to see what regulations might apply where you are) and please use as little of it as possible – see page 32. If you choose to print, stamp or label it with your logo, your packaging will remind the customer – and tell other people who see it – where that otherwise visually generic croissant came from.

Advertising

You might think along the lines of, I shouldn't need to advertise – my Real Bread is the best for miles around and sells itself! That may be so but thinking this way can limit your sales. Even if every trier becomes a buyer, people need to know there's a baker whose loaves are there to be tried. Word of mouth is a brilliant (perhaps the best) form of advertising but it can only reach so far and even your existing customers might still need a gentle nudge from time to time. So dust off your trumpet and pucker up; after all, the supermarket up the road isn't going to blow it for you.

Advertising channels

Means to get your brand known and message across include:

- Knowledgeable, friendly, customer-focussed staff members.
- Virtual shop window (website, social media accounts).
- Mailing list.
- Chalkboard (inside and/or outside the shop).
- Your actual shop window.
- Shelf labels.
- Bread bags.
- Information leaflets.
- Samples.

One of the most trusted, and therefore valuable, means is word of mouth. Encourage your customers to talk, blog, post on social media, leave comments on review sites and otherwise spread the word about what they like about your business and products.

 All marketing must lead to positive word of mouth promotion."

George Casey, Haddie & Trilby, Warwickshire

Differentiation

It pays to let potential (and existing) customers know the reasons for buying loaves from you instead of from someone else. In marketing speak these are your 'points of difference' or your 'USPs' – unique selling points. What makes your business and products different and special? If any of the selling points in this chapter apply (or could be made to apply) to your bakery then SHOUT ABOUT THEM, but at the same time, please leave making false claims to rogue traders.

This is Real Bread

Baking Real Bread could well make you unique in your neighbourhood, so put it up-front in all of your marketing. Even better, sign up to our Real Bread Loaf Mark scheme. Everyone has their own idea of what Real Bread is, so be sure to let people know that yours is in line with the Campaign's definition, ie made without so-called processing aids or other additives. If your own definition narrows this down further (eg only sourdough leavening) then obviously say this as well.

Even a baker(y) using unregulated descriptors like 'craft', 'fresh', 'artisan', 'traditional', 'family-owned' etc doesn't necessarily guarantee that their products are additive-free. We need an Honest Crust Act! In 2009 the chair of the National Association of Master Bakers (since renamed Craft Bakers' Association) in the UK told this book's author that she estimated 80% of their members used additives. While we were updating this book, the CBA was still endorsing the use of additives, accepted advertising and sponsorship from additives suppliers, and backed a proposed code of practice that we see as a sourfaux cheats' charter.

NB We try to avoid criticising individual small bakeries that don't share all of our values. After all, a local, independent business is a good thing. We prefer to encourage them to come round to kicking the additive habit and, where applicable, dropping any disingenuous or potentially misleading marketing. If you ever feel you have a need to make accusations about a fellow small business owner, please first be sure that you have clear proof, then contact them privately to discuss the issue and hear their side of the story. Even if you don't like what you find, please think twice about the possible implications (for you as well as them) of going public.

Sensory appeal

While avoiding straying into any fanciful excesses reminiscent of some wine tasters, how can you accurately and evocatively describe the flavour, aroma, texture of each loaf? Descriptors to be used as appropriate might include: malty, wheaty, nutty, moist, crisp, tangy, roasted, toasted, complex, caramelised, buttery, crackling, flaky, chewy, soft... You might want to have a look at a few so-called artisan loaves in a supermarket and see if there's anything they've paid marketers a fortune to come up with that you can reclaim to use in an honest way.

What's the story?

One way of making a product more interesting and appealing to customers is by telling the story behind it. Threads woven into the story of your bakery or Real Bread that you make might include:

- Landrace, heritage or other non-commodity grain.
- Locally grown wheat (ideally say where and by whom).
- Flour milled locally (name the mill and even the miller?).
- Flour stoneground by wind or water power.
- Other ingredients from farm X or dairy Y.
- Wood-fired oven.

- Traditional local recipe (better if you can qualify 'traditional' with information about its history).
- The only bakery in the area that still makes bread X in a certain way.
- Sourdough or otherwise slowly proved/long-risen.
- Family-owned business.
- Date bakery established, has operated on this site since.
- Bake for/once baked for X (insert major event, well known person or establishment).
- Certified organic business (NB in many countries legal restrictions apply to the use of the O word).
- B Corporation.
- Worker-owned co-operative.
- Community Supported Bakery (see page 55).
- Real Bread Campaign supporter (please join us if you haven't already!).

Better for your community

Is your bakery at the heart of your local community? Is it a business that offers meaningful, skilled jobs to people from your neighbourhood and keeps money circulating in the local economy? Have you helped members of staff gain qualifications or win awards? Is your bakery a place where people, especially older and isolated people, and those who don't visit the local pub (if you're lucky enough to have one) can meet and catch up? Do you do doorstep deliveries and stop for a chat? Do you run a social or community enterprise that gives back, or pays forward, even more to local folk? Don't be shy about saying so in your media work and other marketing.

Promotions

What extra, or different, things can you do from time to time to give shoppers different reasons for buying, and customers extra incentive to keep coming back for more?

Ring the changes

Variety is the spice of life and alongside 'free', the word 'new' is one of the most attention-grabbing in marketing. Are you able to bake a special loaf, either for holidays/festivals and other special occasions, or perhaps every week/month?

Rewarding loyalty

Here are some ways that you might choose to say thanks to frequent or regular customers:

Loyalty card Y'know, like a lot of coffee shops do. With (loaf-shaped?) spaces for you to stamp each time the customer makes an applicable purchase within a given period. Once the card is full, the customer gets a free product. Maybe you do a baker's dozen – buy 12 loaves get one free.

Sneaky bun Every now and then, maybe you throw in a bun or a pastry with a purchase by a frequent customer.

Food co-op discount In return for a local food-buying co-op placing a regular bulk order for a single pick up/delivery, offer a preferential discount. This sort of arrangement will help to make affordable loaves available, while maintaining steady income for your business. See page 66 for more on food co-ops.

Subscription payment discount A customer paying upfront for a regular order gets a discount on the standard, impulse-buy price. This may be proportional to the size of order (eg a greater per-loaf discount for a one month subscription of five loaves a week than for one loaf a week) or length of commitment, eg payment for six months in advance might be discounted more than a monthly subscription.

Reaching out

Whether it's a stand-alone event or part of something wider, a Real Bread activity is a great way to bring people together. After all, the word companion is derived from cum panis, Latin for 'with bread'. As well as making you feel all warm and fuzzy, events and activities that establish and build upon links with your local community are all part of the marketing mix that will help promote your business. Here are some ideas:

Food co-ops

Could you supply or help to run a local food co-op? It's a good way of getting affordable, healthy, real food to people who might otherwise have difficulty accessing it. Find out more on page 66.

Flour show

What local event is complete without some sort of baking competition? As the local expert baker, why not offer to help organise, or at least judge, one? From village fete to harvest festival to food fair, inviting people to roll up their sleeves and make loaves at home to enter in given categories is a great way to get people joining in a friendly competition with tasty results. Whether you have public or closed judging is up to you, though watching people nibble on 20 different loaves for an hour is perhaps a spectator sport only for die-hard bread fans, and can inhibit a full and frank exchange of views between judges.

Bread classes and courses

Running one-off classes or longer courses can not only help to establish links with other people in your local community but also can be a valuable source of income. It can also be another way of helping people on low- to no-incomes access affordable healthy food. You might choose simply to run affordable classes in basic bread making or, as you get suitably experienced and knowledgeable, run 'lifestyle' classes that help to subsidise affordable – or even free – community classes. Anecdotally, several bakers have told us that the more some people learn and understand about bread making, the more likely they are to be loyal customers, who better appreciate what they're paying for.

Bake Your Lawn and Lessons in Loaf

These are Real Bread Campaign initiatives to help children learn about the Real Bread journey from seed to sandwich. They aren't PR stunts, but some bakers have reported that the hands-on experience has helped to create junior Real Bread converts, who dispatch their pester-powered parents to the bakery for more. Guides are available to download from our website and one day might even evolve into our third book.

> » www.sustainweb.org/realbread/books

Together We Rise

As you know yourself, making bread is so therapeutic. Could you team up with a local mental health care provider or community organisation to design mindful or therapeutic bread making sessions? Are there potential local partnerships that could lead to work with people facing other challenges, be they physical (eg stroke, injury, disability), learning difficulties and/or disability, isolation or those associated with aging? Again, any PR from this should be treated as an extra benefit, not the main reason you're doing it. See also the section on social enterprise on page 51.

Bread making at events

Baking in a portable oven is a useful marketing opportunity, helping you to reach potential new customers. Pizzas are a great option as:

- They are quick to make and bake.
- Even when sold at a very affordable price, they have a good profit margin.
- You can involve kids (and others) in shaping and topping their own bases, perhaps even going as far as making the dough.

If customers are involved, you need to follow the food hygiene and event safety guidance that's applicable where you are. If customers make dough, you should provide containers for them to take this home and make the pizzas to be eaten from dough proved in advance.

Team local

How can you and other local businesses support each other?

- A local Real Bread map or tour: if there's more than one Real Bread bakery within walking distance, work together to organise a tasting tour of your top products, or create a map (and perhaps even a voucher) for people to sample the baked delights in their own time. If you're even luckier and have a wheat grower and traditional mill round your way, you could even lead people on the whole trail from seed to sandwich.
- If yours is the only bakery, then how about doing something similar with other local producers and eateries that share your spirit and values?
- Team up for a talk and feast (or whole festival) of Real Bread and whatever great food and drink is crafted by other small batch producers – and produced by local growers – in your area, such as real ale, real cider, artisan cheese, sausages, seasonal fruit and veg, charcuterie and so on.
- Organise a picnic for people in your community.

Are there any local groups of people with similar interests you could join or work with eg a local food partnership/network, Slow Food group, chamber of commerce, local traders' association, Women's Institute, community recycling network etc? In the UK have a look at the Sustainable Food Places website to see if you're in one.

» www.sustainablefoodplaces.org

Big up the little baker

Make sure that your wholesale customers proclaim produce provenance with pride so that their customers know where to buy more of the same for home. Far too many pub, restaurant, café and food van menus we've seen list 'local sourdough bread', 'artisan brioche bun' or similar without naming the bakery. Work to help eateries understand the benefit of including producers' names (perhaps even a section with a line or two about each) on their menus, especially if they charge premium prices, so people know what they're getting isn't just some additive-laden, bake-off product from a factory via a national wholesaler.

Other community activities

- To mark a particular local event, bake a special local loaf, ideally with flour that has been milled locally.
- Run a bread making class for a local community group – WI, youth centre, Scouts/Guides, pub regulars, religious group etc.
- Invite locals to visit the bakery to see it in action.
- Offer deliveries to older, less mobile or isolated people at Christmas, winter, or perhaps year-round.
- Revive a local traditional loaf recipe to bake.
- A harvest festival with Real Bread as the star of the show.

If your cultural heritage is different from that of many people in your neighbourhood, would you like to run an event to help them learn about breads from your culture? If your heritage is of the culture dominant where you are, but there are people in your local community with different national/ethnic/cultural heritage, maybe you can work with people from a particular background to run an event. This could involve a talk and tasting and maybe even making. You could even work together to throw in other food, music and dance to make it a feast or full-on festival.

Websites

Where do people go when they want to find a local supplier of something? For many years, local newspaper classified ads, a phone book or The Yellow Pages were the go-to directories. For many people now an internet search engine is the only place to start.

An internet presence is essential for almost any business looking to communicate with potential customers. A website can be a low-cost form of advertising, which can be tailored to suit the needs of your bakery – from a very basic, one-page 'who, what, where' listing to an all-singing, all-dancing online store.

Unlike physical media (eg posters and leaflets), you can update your online information at the drop of a hat as often as you like for little or no cost. You can provide a rich experience for visitors by including background information and frequently updated photos, news/blog posts and even videos, giving them reasons to linger on the site and return in future.

The best place to find advice about creating and using websites is... you've guessed it: on the internet. Various business advice services, such as Business Link, provide helpful guides to managing online marketing. For examples of the different ways that Real Bread bakeries design, structure and use their websites, pick a few from the Real Bread Map on our site and take a look.

Considerations when setting up a website

There are many things to consider when entering the online world. Your budget and time are two of the biggest factors. If you have no budget for a website but have good IT know-how (or you know someone who does) you can create an impressive website in minutes for next to nothing. However, if you are new to website design, you may want to consult a web designing service.

Other important considerations include:

- **Domain name:** ideally this should be short and memorable – probably your business name, or closely and obviously related to it. You will have to pay to register this, which you can do through an internet service provider.
- **Content:** do you want your website to have a simple listing with basic information about your business and contact details or do you want something more sophisticated?
- **Internet service provider (ISP):** how much does each charge and what support and other services do you get in return?
- **Design:** what will the pages look like? For example, pictures can brighten up your site but too many might leave it looking cluttered.
- **Structure:** how will visitors navigate around the site? It needs to be user-friendly. For example, it's no good hiding your address away somewhere that it would take the user five clicks to find.
- **Testing:** make sure your pages are easy to navigate and all of your links go to

the correct places. Ask your friends or family to try the website and ask for their feedback.

- **Maintenance:** think about how often you will be willing (and able) to update your website content and design that content accordingly. It's no use creating a prominent page for a weekly special loaf on the site if you're not able to update it on a weekly basis, or a page for classes that only has details of a session you ran six months ago.
- **Analytics:** there are many tools available that can help give you a picture of how visitors are using your site, which pages they click on and how long they stay. This can be very useful information to get an idea about what people like about your business and what you could improve.
- **Search engine optimisation (SEO):** ensure that the wording used on your site (on-screen and the hidden tags) match the keywords and phrases people are likely to use when searching for Real Bread. These might include, for instance, 'local bakery', 'bread' or 'sourdough'. SEO also includes raising your search engine ranking – ie how high up the list you come when someone performs a relevant search. Some of the search engines themselves provide information on SEO, as might your ISP or web designer.
- **Online advertising:** you may consider using search engine advertising tools (for example, Google Adwords) to boost the number of visitors to your site. One downside is that you can end up with unwanted advertisers on your site.
- **Who'll do the work?** Do you choose a site builder platform (eg wix.com) with templates and tools that enable you to create and maintain your own site, have a tech-savvy family member or mate who can help out, or do you pay a professional to take care of all that for you?

Blogs

A popular way of getting a very basic web presence in a matter of minutes is a blog, which is short for web log. Blogs are usually free to set up, have ready-to-use design templates and can be mastered by anyone who is comfortable with word processing. Whether you set a blog up with information and images that you change relatively infrequently, use as an online diary/newsletter/soapbox, or a combination of the two, is up to you. You can even include a message board to allow on-screen interaction with customers.

Popular blogging platforms include:

- » www.blogger.com
- » www.wordpress.com
- » www.typepad.com

Making yourself known

Back in 2010, East West Bakery founder Sue Tennyson, shared these thoughts:

Setting up in Arundel – a very conservative town in West Sussex, England – was a challenge. We gave out loads of free tasters, had pictures of our bakers at work in the shop to personalise the product and make connections with producers for the customers. The bakers came into the shop on Saturdays (after a night shift – so complete with baggy eyes!) to reinforce the message that these were the people who stay up all night to make this for you – it proved to be a successful strategy!

We got the local restaurants using our bread and naming us as suppliers on the menu (lots of persuasion and a free beer worked wonders). I also spent a lot of time sending press releases to local and foodie magazines which were then displayed in the shop and we got prominent local folk on side – the movers and shakers of Arundel. Shameless, I know, but it works.

Look for natural allies – places where people are already shopping for quality food and can just pop a loaf in too. We forged links with (and sold loaves through) local organic veg box schemes and sold our bread through other specialist food stores – delis, a partnership with a cake shop, high class butchers, specialist cheese shops...

We did a lot of other things too, including:

- Asking and giving customers what they wanted – they are what it's all about, so we were very hot on customer satisfaction. We asked for, and more importantly responded to, their feedback about what they liked and didn't like.
- Subscribing to specialist food magazines to keep up to date with trends – and sending press releases to them.
- Running cookery classes with kids from local schools at local foodie events and classes for Slow Food – again a natural ally. Is there a group near your bakery?
- Networking like crazy – joining local business groups, Slow Food Brighton, Brighton Food Partnership, Whitehawk Community Food Project, among others.

Social media

Many businesses, large and small, find social media useful for establishing and maintaining real-life relationships, whether they are with customers, suppliers or people in traditional media – TV, newspapers and radio.

Starting a business can be a stressful and isolating experience. Social media platforms also allow bakers to discover and make contact with others around the world to find and share advice, information and inspiration. The Real Bread Campaign, many of our supporters, and individuals and businesses in our wider network of friends are frequent users of social media sites.

 In the early days, we moved from a borrowed kitchen to my home kitchen to another borrowed space. The only fixed points were our mission and our online presence."

Simon Cobb, Stoneham Bakehouse, East Sussex

An important feature of social media platforms is the inclusive nature of the creation and sharing of content – anyone with internet access can get involved. The information you make available through such channels can be text, images, audio or video. With many services, you have the choice of allowing anyone to read what you post or limiting access to a particular group of contacts. They also allow you to send and receive direct/private messages, a bit like mini emails.

How do I use my social media account(s)?

It's important to contribute by creating and updating your content so that people want to return to visit your profile again. This could be in the form of recipes, pictures, events, interesting news or video clips. You should also remember that social media is not all 'me, me, me', it's a space for conversation – interaction in order to strengthen and enlarge your online relationships. Don't just broadcast your own information; if you see something interesting that someone else has posted, repost, like, and comment on it. All social media sites publish guides on how and why to use them and there are many more unofficial guides published by users.

Hashtags

The internet age has revived and repurposed the archaic #, AKA the octothorp and (mainly by Americans) the pound sign.* Attached to the front of a word, or other unbroken string of characters, the hashtag allows users to search for social media posts that contain that word. While some people use hashtags for commentary (eg #WhatWasIThinking #SorryNotSorry) they can be useful in helping your message reach more people than just your current followers/friends.

Bakery-related hashtags that you might find useful (as appropriate) include: #RealBread #RealBreadWeek #bread #baking #bakery #microbakery #LocalFood #HomeBaking #HomeBaker #SmallBusiness #BakersLife #ArtisanBread #ArtisanBaker #sourdough #BakersOfColor #BlackBakers #LocalBakery #WeAreRealBread #NaturallyLeavened #SourdoughStarter. Look for and use geographically-associated tags (eg #YorkshireHour #NobHill #StKilda) that can be useful for making your posts visible to, and helping you connect with, more people in your area than just your followers and fellow breadheads.

Some hashtags are platform-specific (eg: #InstaBread #BakersOfInstagram #IGBreadClub #InstaFood #Breadstagram) and some platforms have limits to how many hashtags you can include in a post.

*Nerds like your author here may be interested to look up its origins, which some experts believe can be traced back to ℔, a version of the lb abbreviation for the Roman libra pondo, ie a pound in weight.

Social media platforms

These come and go (MySpace and Friends Reunited, anyone?) but three of those that were around when we wrote the first edition of this book that are still going strong are Facebook, Instagram and Twitter. We'll leave it to you to research and satisfy yourself about the various ethical questions raised around each...

Facebook

Can be used to set up personal profiles, as well as pages or groups for organisations. It allows users to publish details of events and upload pictures, has a notice board (referred to as a wall) on which the user and others can post messages, and allows users to send messages to others (referred to as friends or fans). Good for making connections with local customers. If you're hesitant to build your own standalone website, a Facebook page can effectively act as a basic one. It's a place where you can publish essential details about your business, your story and news updates and even set up a basic online shop.

Instagram

An image-led platform (each post must contain a photo or video) ideally suited to visually appealing food. This superficial basis, however, means that there is a tendency for people to like a post without actually reading the content. If you don't have an image that catches people's eye, your post could be overlooked by many, no matter how amazing your bread, or important your message, is. URLs in posts don't become active hyperlinks, so you have to put them in your Insta profile.

Twitter

A quick and succinct way of communicating messages of up to 280 characters, which can include a hyperlink – eg to your website. Can be used for polls and short conversations. We've found that the use of Twitter by people in our existing community is in decline in favour of the other two platforms above.

 Twitter and Facebook can give you an immediate response from customers. Many food writers and journalists use Twitter so it can be an excellent way of making contacts and getting your brand across to influential people."

Peter Cook, Peter Cooks Bread, Herefordshire

Media relations

Strong media relations can make the difference between your bakery being the one that is known, trusted and consequently frequented by people from miles around, or completely unheard of by anyone other than a small band of regular customers and the odd passer-by.

Unless your turnover is large enough to support contracting a media/public relations agency, this is something that you will need to look after yourself.

What and why?

As the name suggests, media relations (AKA public relations or PR) is about building relationships with relevant journalists, editors, broadcasters and bloggers so that when you have a story to tell, they are more likely to help you spread the word. It also means that when they are putting together a relevant news story or feature and need an interview, case study or picture, you are the first person/company that springs to mind. Two of the key benefits of a news piece or feature in the local media as opposed to an advertisement are:

- Research suggests people see articles as independent and trustworthy opinions and therefore of greater marketing value.
- Other than any fee you pay to a PR agency, it's free!

Even if you feel you do not need the help of media coverage to help maintain and grow your business, at the very least consider having on file a general background release – see below. You then have this available for reactive PR – a local media outlet asks you for information because they're doing a story about Real Bread Week and want to mention a local bakery, for example.

Dark arts?

This area of marketing is one that some small business owners overlook, or dismiss as too time-consuming, outside their skillset or simply irrelevant. Based upon a perception of 'spin doctors' covering up negative stories, or putting out misleading information, some people even see PR as 'bad'. PR is simply a set of tools with no inherent values, though. Just as a knife can be used to harm, craft or heal, it is the intent and action of a person whether or not PR is used for positive or negative purposes.

Media release

A media release (also known as a press release) is a very useful tool in persuading newspapers, magazines, TV/radio programmes and bloggers to help you communicate your messages to members of the public.

The pitch

Different people look for different things, depending on factors including the topics they cover (environment, rural, small business, local news etc), their patch (local, regional, national, international), whether they cover things from a news or features angle, the outlet/publication and its audience. You won't appeal to everyone every time you have something to say, but even modest media interest can lead to good coverage of your story.

To increase the chances of local media coverage, ask yourself why someone would be interested in your story. What makes it stand out? Is it something new, different (eg reviving ancient traditions or making/doing something that nobody else in the area does), local (eg using only locally-grown landrace wheat), of benefit to people in your local community (eg fundraising for a charity), or bringing local relevance to a wider issue – joining in with a national or international event or movement, such as initiatives run by the Real Bread Campaign?

Considerations

Before you knuckle down to craft your media release, think:

- **Purpose** Why am I sending it? What do I want to achieve?
- What are the **key points** of what I am trying to communicate?
- Who is my target **audience**?
- What's my **hook**, the stand-out, attention-grabbing element?
- When is the right **time** to send it?
- Is a media release **the best means** by which to communicate this message to this audience and to achieve what I want?

Purpose

Getting media coverage is rarely – if ever – an end in itself; it's the means to an end. The actual purpose of getting coverage might be:

- People buying X or booking places in your new baking class.
- Crowdfunding your new bakery.
- Other action – eg writing to your MP to save the local community hub in which the bakery is located.
- A bump to ongoing general awareness-raising for your business.

On this last point, you might feel that a local website is unlikely to cover the launch of your new doughnut (though you never know…) but the purpose was really to keep you in the site editor's mind for the next time they need an expert commentator.

Key points

What are the Ws (and an H) – the what, when, where, why, who and how – of the story?

Audience

Think about the audience of the publications (and particular columns/sections within them) to which you are sending the release and write for that audience.

With whom are you attempting to connect? An older person who might like the idea of a traditional, local tearoom selling amazing crumpets? A businessperson for whom a free-range bacon sarnie on Real Bread on the way to work may be attractive? A parent who'd be happy to pay you to take the kids off their hands for an afternoon of bread making in the school holidays? Think also of each publication/outlet and the sections within it you're hoping will cover your story – what angles do they take on things?

Ideally, you'd tailor releases for every single recipient. Although this is not possible, if you're targeting different press sectors (eg local news, environment, community, rural affairs, bakery trade press, small business news, foodie press) with the same story, try to at least write adapted versions, rather than issuing one catch-all release.

The hook

What element or angle will give your release the best chance of being picked by an editor/journalist as being of special interest to their audience? Is what you're talking about:

- New or the first time something's happened?
- Significantly different?
- Of particular benefit to the audience of the publication in question?
- Making a wider issue relevant to a particular group of people – eg enabling local people to participate in a national or international event or movement?
- Of human interest? For example, what you are doing is helping someone face or overcome a challenge in life. Only to be considered if there is a genuine connection and can be done in a non-exploitative way with full consent of the person/people whose story/life intersects with what you are doing.
- Linked to a celebrity? Wrongly or rightly, many media types – and their audiences – are more (or only) interested in a story if there's a celebrity connection. If you have a customer who is well known locally or beyond, and this is a route you're comfortable taking, you could ask them if they'd be happy to be involved somehow eg turning up for a photo opportunity, giving a supportive quote, or at least endorsing whatever it is and letting you use their name.

Timing

Old news is no news: news happens now. The time to put out a news release is as soon as you have a story to tell. This might be before it has happened (we're launching our new therapeutic baking classes next month) or immediately afterwards (yesterday we raised £10,000 for the local hospice).

Features generally don't have the same time pressures, allowing research and interviews to be carried out over a longer period. The window might still not be open all year round, though – a publication is unlikely to be interested in your hot cross buns in September.

Everyone has a deadline for submission and publication. For example, a website might have a daily cut-off and a local weekly paper might work a few days ahead of publication. Weekly national supplements might have deadlines a month ahead, while glossy monthlies can plan three to six months in advance. For some, the time for pulling together Christmas editions, supplements and guides is June and July. Research the deadlines of the media you are targeting to make sure you don't miss them.

If you have set a date/time before which you don't want a story to be published/broadcast, mark the release with details eg "Embargoed until 9am, 20 December." Embargoes are not legally binding but most journalists will respect them. Don't bother though if it really isn't time sensitive.

Content and structure

Keep it as short as possible and only as detailed as necessary. The person reading your release probably will have an inbox full of them and be hardened against waffle by years of experience, so cut to the chase and leave out unnecessary fluff and hyperbole. If they get to paragraph two or three and you still haven't hit them with the key points, well they probably won't have read as far as paragraph two or three.

A media release has three main parts: headline, lead and body.

Headline

First impressions count. This is your one-line pitch to capture the attention of the reader and act as bait to make them continue. Get this wrong and they might not even open the email. No pressure, then.

If possible, the headline should be a snappy summary of what you are about to say in as few words as possible. Where the content of the message is lighter in nature, wit might help your release to stand out, in which case the use of dreadful puns is a matter of personal choice.

Lead

You've hooked the reader, now reel 'em in with a short paragraph containing all the Ws (oh, and an H) of the story: the what, why, where, when, who and how. The saying 'don't bury the lead' means get your key points in here, rather than bury them further down. Keep to the facts and write no more than one or two lines, or bullet points, of up to about 50 words in total.

Body

Use the rest of your release to expand on the points you outlined in the lead paragraph. Organise information from most important at the beginning through to progressively less important information further down – the least important shouldn't even make it onto the release.

- What is the most important fact you need to get across?
- Are there any unique or otherwise truly newsworthy aspects of your event, announcement, activity, product or service?
- Is there a financial aspect? If it's positive (eg a significant discount or free anything) put it high up in the release, perhaps even in the headline.

If your news story is the latest episode of a long saga, or has a complex background, include a short recap towards the end of the release to summarise the key points to date. Alternatively, these can be included in notes to editors after the release.

Quotes

Journalists and the rest of us love to hear/read people's voices. To give the release, and coverage it hopefully will help to generate, a human touch, include a short quote. This could be a notable person (such as a trusted expert, local figure or celebrity) or the business owner, which might well be you.

Images

'A picture paints...' and all that. If you have taken or commissioned a strong, high quality photo (see notes below), include it with the release as it can be the visual hook that helps to 'sell' your story to the editor. Alternatively, add a note after the body saying that images are available on request.

If what you are talking about might create a photo opportunity eg a celebrity, an opening, an eye-catching event or an unusual setting or prop, then make sure you highlight this. If the opportunity is particularly interesting, then it is worth writing a shorter release containing the when, where, what (and who) of the occasion, inviting newspaper and other media picture desks to take their own photos.

Format

- People in the media receive an endless stream of releases, so keep yours short and punchy. Ideally, try to say what you need to in 300-500 words. If a writer or editor needs/wants more, they'll ask.
- Ensure that your writing is clear, concise, and without jargon.
- Write about yourself in the third person: say 'the bakery' rather than 'we' (except in direct quotes).
- If sending by post or emailing as an attachment, the best format is A4 with borders of at least 2cm all around.
- Text should be 11-12 points and double spaced.

- Font is a matter of choice but for ease of reading (and to be taken seriously) avoid cartoony or script fonts.
- After the body copy, insert the word ENDS.
- After this, include the date of the release, name and contact details (phone and/or email) for more information. If images or interviews are available, say so.

An optional final inclusion is 'Note(s) to the editor'. This is a summary of key facts that either are spread out through the release, or relevant background information that does not appear in it - eg a potted history of the bakery and any awards it has won.

Accuracy

A few very important points:

- Double-check for spelling mistakes or other errors that a spellchecker wouldn't pick up on - eg a correctly spelt word but in the wrong place.
- Check your punctuation and grammar.
- Make sure that all of your facts (like dates and names) and contact details are correct and that any sources are quoted correctly.
- Even if you've read it ten times yourself, always ask someone else to proofread before sending.

The right contact

Although you are undoubtedly extremely busy running your business, it's worth taking a little time to find out the right contact at your local newspaper, news website, radio or TV station.

Research the subjects covered by particular TV stations, websites, radio stations and shows/sections within each. You also need to find the right person (or desk) to send the release to. The right contact depends on a number of factors, including the type of story you have, how many staff a publication/station has and how that organisation divides up its workload.

The news editor Might have business news or local events in their remit.

The features editor Might be interested in doing a profile on a long-running family business, recently started business or business that's doing something in an interesting/unusual way.

Features writer Might be easier to get hold of than the features editor.

Food editor Some food editors only work on recipes, others cover food-related features and/or news.

Forward planning desk TV and radio stations usually have a person/team who note(s) details of events in a diary long in advance. If they are interested, they then contact you close (often very close) to the event to arrange to cover the story.

The editor Smaller publications might not have features, news or food editors, so the editor might be the key point of contact who will then pass the story to the relevant journalist.

The deputy editor Can often be easier to get hold of than the editor.

Specialist desk Are there dedicated reporters for business, rural affairs, local events, environment or other relevant area?

Building relationships

Establishing and building a relationship with the right contact can lead to being featured again. Don't expect a weekly column, but out of sight is out of mind and if you're known to a journalist or editor, there is more of a chance that he/she will think of you if a comment or example is needed for a related article in the future.

Post or email?

It's quick and easy to delete an email, but then it's also quick and easy to read one. Emails are also cheap to send and use no paper. The preference for receiving press releases by post or email varies from person to person – it pays to find out what each of your contacts prefers, especially if you are only sending your release to a few. Since the first edition of this book, email has become the norm, so a dead tree technology media release arriving by snail mail might make it stand out.

Follow up

Some stories have a life of their own – you send a release out and it flies, but these are the exception. Securing coverage often involves following up the release with a phone call. Some journalists can get tetchy about this, being of the 'I read everything and will be in touch if I need to know more' school, though many are happy to chat briefly.

Trade press

Generally, media interest in news such as a new staff member, refit of the bakehouse or trading results, will be limited to baking industry trade press, and perhaps local business news journalists. Trade releases can be even shorter and less prosaic than media releases to consumer press.

General background release

To save time having to repeat details of your business to editors/writers, it is useful to have a short, up to date, general overview that you can send out when needed. This only needs to be a few paragraphs, summing up details such as:

- A brief history of the bakery.
- Who the owners are.
- A mini-biography of the head/only baker – including any previous bakeries worked at.
- Any significant awards won.
- Future plans.
- Contact details.

Photos and copyright

Consider commissioning a photographer to take a selection of pictures for you to keep on file - eg interior and exterior shots of the bakery, photos of the owner/s and head/only baker, and maybe a few product shots. If you have obtained photos in another way (eg ones a photographer took for a local paper/magazine) be sure you have the copyright holder's permission to use them and how. For example, they may be happy for you to use a photo on your own website or social media but not to send them to another publication. Don't lift images from the internet: they are likely to be subject to copyright and even if they aren't, picture editors tend only to use generic or third-party shots that they have sourced for themselves.

Give us a plug

Whenever the opportunity arises, we'd love it if you gave the Real Bread Campaign a mention, please. If you're a paid-up Campaign supporter, please say so.

Let us know

If a media outlet picks up your story, please let us know. We'd love to share news of your success with others. If it's online, please email a link to: realbread@sustainweb.org.

Alternatives

Is sending out a media release the best way to achieve what you are trying to do? Is it the best means through which to communicate whatever the message is to whoever you want to receive it? Alternative channels include:

- Your website.
- An e-newsletter to people on your mailing list.
- Social media accounts.
- Talking face-to-face – eg in your shop, at your market stall, at a food festival or other local event.
- Leaflets/flyers.
- Print, digital, radio or ambient (eg on bus shelters) adverts.
- Picking up the phone.

Scaling up your business

You're gonna need a bigger boat...

Whatever your original plans, you might find that you need to expand your bakehouse (either by extension or moving to new premises) at least once. Ideally, you will have included this in your original business plan. So, where to next?

 Running quite a big wholesale operation from home was not sustainable in the long run. We always knew that it was a stepping stone to opening a bakery, which happened as soon as we had the funds and the perfect location."

Adam Pagor, Grain and Hearth, Whitstable

General considerations

When renting, buying (or even building) a new bakehouse, you need to allow enough space not only for the original level of production, but also for whatever level of expansion you plan in at least the short to mid-term. Don't go over the top and buy an aircraft hangar, but bear in mind it is easier to expand a business within a space than move to a new one. Things to think about when planning your move might include:

- Storage areas for ingredients should have easy access for receiving heavy deliveries, such as sacks of flour. Preferably they should be on the ground floor or have a lift.
- Space adjacent to the bakery for suppliers to park, or stop temporarily, legally (and ideally without a charge) when making deliveries, and perhaps also for customers.
- Staff toilets.
- Ventilation for the oven and production area in general. Planning permission may be required for an exhaust system, which will have to comply with building regulations. Your local authority will be able to advise.
- People. In addition to dedicated toilets, your team needs space for breaks and to store their non-work clothing and other personal items securely. You might also factor in kitchen (or at least tea and coffee making) facilities.

- Access – eg ramps for wheelchairs and pushchairs.
- Public transport options, and cycle parking, for staff and customers who don't drive.
- Any planned or potential pedestrianisation of a high street: it can help to make or break businesses.
- Property owner or local authority requirements and restrictions, eg regarding signage.
- The bins! Where will you store recyclables and waste before collection?

You might find that your main equipment supplier offers a planning and design service. This could perhaps include things like producing building floor plans and elevations, showing the proposed details on architects' drawings, as well as detailed technical specifications for submission to a local authority requesting information on ventilation systems, odour and noise control measures etc.

> Whatever space you think you need to start with, at least double it as you'll generally very quickly find that space becomes an issue. Moving a bakery can be a very expensive exercise."
>
> *Troels Bendix, The Hungry Guest, West Sussex*

> How you utilise space is key. Rather than moving, I have increased capacity by good use of vertical space. If well planned, smaller spaces can be very efficient and the baker may actually spend less time running around. You can also increase production by working in a systematic way with a clean-as-you-go approach."
>
> *Ian Waterland, Knead Good Bread, Leicestershire*

No one ever said it was gonna be easy

Journeyman baker, and former Campaign ambassador, Aidan Chapman said: "Becoming a Real Bread baker is a lifestyle, not a career choice." Troels Bendix, who has also set up and worked in a number of successful bakeries, expanded on this point: "One thing I must emphasise: opening a bakery is such a commitment. In the process many will find out how difficult it is to make money this way. Baking is anything but glamorous. It nearly killed me! You cannot think by going on a course or reading some books that you are prepared. You will learn in time and get better in time. But be prepared to suffer lots of nights with little or no sleep, a decrease in social life or a lack of money. Is it worth it and would I do it again? Hell yeah!"

High street shop

If you're ready to make the leap, you might look for a shop on a high street with plenty of passing potential customers. If you're lucky, you'll find a building ready to fit out as your bakery. Others will need more investment and work. If you're planning to convert a building from one use to another (eg from residential, office or different food/retail) check with your local authority if permission is required. Considerations before setting up (or taking on) a retail bakery shop/space include:

- The cost of buying or renting the building.
- The cost of fitting out the bakehouse and shop to meet your needs.
- Finding, keeping and managing staff.
- Other overheads, including salaries, insurance, maintenance, repairs, energy bills, local taxes and service charges.
- Whether there is enough demand locally to generate income that will cover these costs and turn a profit.
- Its location – will there be enough passing custom for what you plan to sell?

The rent and business rates on retail space can be significant, as can the cost of waste and recycling collections, but these vary according to factors including the local authority, property owner and location. Costs will differ between a small village and a large city, and perhaps even between one end or side of a street and the other. Shop around to find the most viable option.

Investigate whether there are plans to start, or regenerate, a retail area locally. If so, the local authority or developer may be offering below-market rent/rates to attract tenants. Local business owners (perhaps even a chamber of commerce or other traders' association) may be able to provide valuable insight and advice about operating in the location(s) you're considering.

Haddie & Trilby founder George Casey suggested questioning whether a high street shop is best, or even right, for your business: "You don't necessarily need an expensive, high footfall location. You might be wasting money on rent. High footfall also equals high rates, which may mean nearly doubling the building's costs. Concentrate on making the product excellent and, if word of mouth is strong, people will find you. If your product is not good, it doesn't matter where you are!"

Industrial estate unit

This option is more suitable for a wholesale business and/or as a central bakery that supplies a number of retail outlets you run in the local area, rather than having a bakehouse in each. Such units offer lots of uninterrupted space – no cramming stuff in nooks and crannies or running up and down stairs between storage and production areas. Maybe you could set up your own mill on site, too? They also tend to have a lower rent per square foot/metre than bakehouse space in high street shops or units in other retail settings. On the downside, they are often in remote places, perhaps served poorly (if at all) by public transport. This can create a challenge for staff members and – if the site owner permits you to make retail sales at your unit – customers. Industrial units can also be very cold in winter and very hot in summer.

Railway arch

Spacious, accessible and often close to a train station or other transport links, spaces under rail lines can work well as bakeries. You may need to arrange having supplies (electricity, gas, water, sewage) installed or upgraded, invest in having the arch lined and doors built for one or both ends. Rail arches are prone to noise, vibrations, damp, cold and vermin, from which you'll need to protect your staff members, equipment, ingredients and – if you set up a shop or café – customers.

In 2019, Network Rail in the UK sold off many of its railway arches. A report from the public accounts committee criticised the deal for a lack of certainty about protection from unfair rental increases and other tenants' rights, as well as questioning the longer-term cost/value of the sale to taxpayers. We have heard a number of negative reports about the arches' new owners from bakers.

On a farm

A suitably renovated and converted outbuilding on a farm might have similar pros and cons to an industrial estate unit. Added potential benefits might include a thriving farm shop on site, through which you can sell your loaves, and perhaps the opportunity to use – and maybe even mill – grain grown on your doorstep.

Shipping container

In 2021, Birch Bread founder Lucie Steel wrote an article for our True Loaf magazine on her years as a shipping container microbaker. Here are some of her top tips:

Planning Speak to your local authority planning department before you order one.

Size Go as large as you can afford. What looks huge to begin with will very quickly seem very small! It's pretty snug inside, so plan your space carefully and all things are possible. Measure very carefully before ordering equipment and make sure you can fit everything through the door. Double doors at one end makes it easier to get big bits of kit in and out, but can limit how you lay out your space.

Shell or shell out You can buy an empty shell very cheaply and do it all yourself, or pay more for a container already fitted out.

Utilities Make sure you factor in the cost of hooking up electricity, water, waste water and maybe also gas. Get onsite quotes for installation and then get your chosen installers booked in well ahead of when you'll need them.

Location Measure your site carefully to be sure the container will fit and check that a small lorry crane can offload it to the exact spot. Seek advice as to what, if any, foundations you might need.

Heat and moisture You will need an extraction system or at least very good ventilation. Make sure your fridge has as much ventilation as possible. Be prepared to insulate the outside of your container as well as the inside. It is HOT in the summer and COLD in the winter.

Storage As space is very limited, you may need to store flour elsewhere, such as a garden shed or garage. Invest in sturdy, watertight and rodent-proof containers that each holds an unopened 25kg flour sack, rather than having to decant it.

Lucie added: "If after a few years your circumstances change or you simply decide microbakery's not for you, your shipping container should have a good secondhand value. That is unless someone else in your family sees it as a potential new shed and moves their stuff in!"

Shared space

On their way to bakehouses of their own, some bakers have perched on the stepping stone of sharing a space with others. In their early days, The Dusty Knuckle, E5 Bakehouse, and The Handmade Bakery had start-up stints in other businesses' kitchens. At Jamie Oliver's original Fifteen restaurant in east London, Real Bread bakers used to take over the kitchen in the hours between the evening shift clearing down and the breakfast shift clocking on.

A local pizzeria (or other eatery) owner might let you use their kitchen and oven overnight or at another time when they're not using it. Perhaps a mill, pub, church or community hall has an oven you could use, or would allow you to rent a back room in which to set one up.

Had Lisa Stockton and Happy Kitchen not allowed us to rent part of their production facility, E5 would probably not have been able to start."

Ben Mackinnon, E5 Bakehouse, London

Some potential advantages:

- Rent can be minimal, or perhaps even waived (maybe in return for baked goods), though you should at least offer to contribute to energy costs and other overheads.
- You won't need the same initial capital investment that it takes to open your own place. The kitchen is up and running already and it's likely that you'll share at least some equipment.

Some potential disadvantages:

- Having limited space to store ingredients or equipment, or perhaps even having to take them away between baking sessions.
- Finding places to leave dough to prove that doesn't get in the way of the other users.
- Your ingredients and/or equipment being borrowed or going missing.
- Compromise – you'll have to fit in with a set-up and schedule that's perhaps less than ideal for you and your business.

"We rapidly needed more oven space and started thinking of places that had ovens, like schools and dying pubs, then realised there was an Italian restaurant with a large stone-bottomed pizza oven in the village. We approached the owner, who was very supportive and enthusiastic and let us do some trials. It did the trick for a dozen loaves at a time and we started the subscription scheme, baking twice a week during the day when the restaurant was unused."

Dan McTiernan, The Handmade Bakery, Slaithwaite

"Instantly having a community around us when we first started was good fun, and it taught us to respect the kitchen environment and clear up after ourselves. It also meant that our rent was significantly less than if we had needed to rent a unit alone. However, sharing a space, especially as a growing company, resulted in lots of conflict. In our desperation to keep baking we used Happy Kitchen's gluten-free ovens for our bread. In retaliation they hid our baking trays. Ten years on I'm pleased to say we can laugh about it, but at the time it was an ordeal."

Ben Mackinnon, E5 Bakehouse, London

Food/kitchen incubator

This specialised type of shared space is set up for professional food production or catering and available for short-term rental at reasonable rates. They can be hired for one-off events or for longer as a testing ground for a business. Though it's unlikely you'll find one with a steam-injection three-deck oven, there should be something that'll do the job, possibly along with a suitable mixer and other useful kit. Some offer business training and other support for the budding food entrepreneur.

Wholesale

An alternative (or addition) to selling direct to customers is supplying retailers or food businesses, such as cafés and restaurants. The potential pros of wholesaling include steady cashflow from regular (and possibly sizeable) orders. Against this you will be expected to cut your margin and an order cancelled or account closed can leave a large hole on your balance sheet. Here are some thoughts from Colin Hilder of the All Natural Bakery:

- Look for opportunities with local delis, restaurants, pubs and caterers.
- Make ordering easy for the retailer. Give clear product information with description, ingredients, photographs and a clear list with prices and codes for ordering. Send a current list out regularly – at least monthly and perhaps weekly.
- Distribution costs are potentially deadly for a wholesale business, so try for business from customers geographically close to you at first and then, when you are ready, grow the radius gradually.

> Wholesale usually involves less expense for premises, often being on an industrial estate or in an out-of-the-way place. While at a glance the set-up and running expense is less, there will be the expense of a delivery van and its driver. Further, when you are working with your hands and aspiring to be a craftsman baker, it really hurts to give away that 20-25% that is the accepted wholesale rate."
>
> *Paul Merry, Panary, Dorset*

> Avoid trying to be everything to everyone. You produce the bread you produce so avoid niche orders where you are asked to develop something new unless the quantities are so large that it is worthwhile."
>
> *Romilla Arber, Honesty Group, Berkshire*

> We initially did only retail, then mainly retail with a bit of wholesale and now mainly wholesale with a bit of retail. In the early days when our baking could be quite (very?) inconsistent, retail was much more comfortable as the customer sees the product before deciding to buy, and if you have a flop you're not jeopardising anyone else's income. The wholesale discount and costs of delivery makes a huge difference to your ability to break even. And it rankles when you see a sandwich made with your bread being sold at about two-and-a-half times what you've charged for the whole loaf!"
>
> *Maggie Rich, Companions Real Bread, Bedford*

A trail of breadcrumbs from your kitchen

By Paul Merry, a professional baker since the 1970s, who runs Panary, a baking school and consultancy in Dorset.

Taking the step from being an amateur to a professional baker can be a slow and steady affair, or a big leap. When it is slow and steady it is usually neighbourhood-centred. You start off just baking for a few friends but soon you find yourself providing bread to half your neighbours. Then you get a stall at a local market, your bread is admired and before you know it, you're supplying a village shop or two and your nearby farm shop. If the momentum keeps going, soon you will be challenged to start reducing the hours you do at your normal job.

Often have I been wide-eyed with admiration listening to one of these bakers on the cusp of becoming a professional, describing how they work in their kitchen for a whole day and night before market day, perhaps snatching a couple of hours' sleep before loading the car and heading off to claim their pitch.

The right stuff

Whether you take the giant leap, or gradually emerge as a professional, there are things in common. It helps to have such a passion about bread making that you are forever chasing after 'the perfect loaf'. If you wish to be a craftsman, working with your hands and minimum machinery, in order to become excellent you must have this yearning and aspire to make the best bread you can, day after day, forever chasing excellence. If, on the other hand, you are driven more by the goal of earning a good living, or building a brand/name that you can franchise, then the passion to chase the elusive perfect loaf is not essential in your make-up. Instead you will need the passion to understand and quickly master the nuts and bolts of the business side of high quality, small scale baking.

Start small

In the early days of being a professional baker, I think it is wise to start small. Give yourself time to get the hang of being a baker who is learning skills. By doing the same tasks every day you will gradually increase your efficiency and pick up speed. When the business is going well enough for you to think the workload has become something of a nightmare, employ another baker and/or get more help in the busy shop. I urge the baker to attend some courses, and try to pin down a job for a while in a bakery so that the scale and rhythm of a working bakery can be experienced and understood.

Bakery equipment

This section builds on the one that starts on page 25. As you scale up production, you will need kit of capacity, performance and durability to match. Choose equipment that will help control all of the variables at each stage of production to ensure consistency and make your job easier. Sometimes the old saying 'buy cheap, buy twice' applies, but in other cases something basic and cheap will do the job as well as – if not better than – something that's fancy, built for looks rather than performance, or that has an undeserved brand name premium.

Ask other bakers what they use to get an idea of pros and cons, reliability etc. When buying new, get quotes from more than one supplier. Good bakery equipment companies can be really helpful in helping you pick the right gear for your needs, may have test kitchens to try before you buy larger items, and provide after-sales support that in some cases can include site visits on top of helplines.

Mixer

As you scale up, your arms (and even a domestic mixer) are going to struggle. There are a handful of basic types typically used by Real Bread bakers.

Planetary or stand

Vertical mixers with variable speeds and a choice of attachments (usually beater hook and whisk) that can be used for thin batters right through to stiff doughs. Overmixing is a risk, particularly at high speeds, and friction can cause the dough to heat up. Although not the most efficient type of mixer, a mechanical 'workhorse' with no electronics tends to keep on going, is flexible, and can be fixed using cheap and readily available parts. Some Hobart mixers made in the 1950s (and even before) are still in use, for example.

Spiral

Commonly found in craft bakeries around the world. When buying, check that the bowl and tool are driven by separate motors, then compare the power of the motors. Mike Hampson of equipment supplier Becketts suggested that machine weight is also some indication of durability. Lighter machines, originally developed for pizza restaurants, are available in sizes and prices suitable for smaller bakeries.

Twin arm

Twin arm mixers have a slow action that mimics human arms lifting and stretching dough. The longer mixing time (around double that of a spiral and perhaps six or eight times that of a high-speed mixer) generates less heat than higher speed mixing. The gentle action can be more suitable for weaker flours, such as those common in continental Europe. Perhaps the best known brand is Artofex. Current models have dough capacities from 80-300kg. Second-hand and reconditioned models are available and, like Hobarts, can run for decades – see the note on used equipment below.

Fork

The forked tool folds the dough over itself repeatedly as the bowl rotates, incorporating air. Like twin arm mixers, lower speeds and gentle action means less friction, lower dough temperature and less risk of overmixing.

Oven

 The oven is where to put your money. You can probably manage without everything else for a while but if your oven dies so does your turnover."

George Casey, Haddie & Trilby, Warwickshire

Heat is transferred in three ways:

- Convection: the rise of hot air, which may be modified by a fan.
- Conduction: the transfer of heat through direct contact – mainly from the oven floor/deck to the dough sitting on it.
- Radiation: heat transfer from one object to another by electromagnetic waves. In an oven this is mainly from the walls.

Bakers who use traditional brick or masonry ovens swear that they give the ideal balance of these means of heat transfer and can produce the best bread. Their thick walls are an excellent source of steady radiant heat, heavy sole plates provide a big hit of conducted heat to the base of the dough and their shapes result in optimum convection currents. As Mike Hampson said, however: "Unfortunately, a stone-built oven that takes three days to heat from cold is impractical in most situations."

Deck oven

This is probably the most common type of oven in small-to-medium Real Bread bakeries. It comprises a number of gas or electric ovens (decks) stacked on top of each other. Typically, each deck has a heated stone (more commonly refractory concrete) sole/floor, the temperature of which can be controlled separately from the chamber. In some cases, the heat at the front can be controlled to account for loss from the door opening. Each deck has a front door that flips up to allow products to be loaded in and out. Some have glass doors to allow you to keep an eye on the baking without losing heat, and a steam injection system can usually be added. A small deck oven may hold one standard UK baking sheet (30" x 18"), while larger ones may hold three or more sheets per deck. They are often modular, making it easier to load into a bakery deck by deck and bolt together on site, as well as to add decks at a later date.

Rack oven

This type of oven is more suited to bakeries at the larger end of the small-to-medium scale. It allows a bakery rack to be wheeled straight from one stage of production to the next without any loading and unloading in between.

Prover and retarder

These allow you to control the temperature and humidity for holding dough between mixing and baking, so it's ready when you need it, rather than when the seasonally fluctuating temperature of your bakery decrees. Provers (more commonly called proofers in the USA) operate at optimum proving temperature or higher, while retarders keep the dough cool to slow fermentation. As the name suggests, the temperature range of a retarder-prover allows it to do both jobs. A timer allows it to switch from chilling dough, perhaps at the end of an evening shift, to proving it in time for the morning shift to bake. Mike Hampson suggested: "As a very rough guide, proving capacity should be two to three times your baking capacity."

Other equipment

Mike Hampson said: "Unless you are absolutely certain you need other pieces of equipment from day one, it is often better to wait to see proof that you do need them, rather than purchasing at the outset. Water meters, dividers, moulders, slicers, wrappers and so on can all be added to the bakery later, as required, to suit your products, output and budget."

Paul Merry of Panary in Dorset noted: "For small scale crafters, remember 'alternative' technology is there for you. You can get superb pastry rollers that have a crank handle, not an electric motor, and there are good manual bun presses available that can stamp out 30-odd buns or rolls at a time without the electric rotating head facility. Actually, hand finished buns and rolls will usually be better than the ones from the electric rotary press, which often manages to mangle them to some degree."

Racks

Because you can't have a bunch of small cake racks lying all around a bakery. Commercial racks can be used to hold baking trays loaded with products before and after baking. Choosing a rack on wheels allows you to move large amounts of products from one part of the bakery to another in one go. It also makes it easier to clean under and around it.

Shelving

No food, or anything containing food (boxes, flour sacks, bowls or proving baskets full of dough etc), should make direct contact with the floor. If you choose units with wire shelves, they can be used as racks for products as they cool.

Storage bins

Typically made from heavy-duty plastic and available on wheels, these can be more practical than having and heaving paper flour sacks around the bakery.

Walk-in fridge

Somewhere between useful and essential if you run a bakery café, catering operation or otherwise make more than just bread. As well as holding vegetables, dairy products, meats or anything else you use that needs refrigeration, a walk-in can also act as a retarder – see above.

Work table/bench

Choose one with an easy to clean surface (see page 108) on a very sturdy frame that will take years of having tens of kilos pummelled on it by strong (and perhaps occasionally grumpy) bakers. Again, wheels make floor cleaning easier.

Second-hand equipment

Some bakeries have relied on ex-display, reconditioned and other used equipment, particularly when starting out. For example, Thoughtful Bakery owner Duncan Glendinning told us that the only new fitting he bought for his original bakehouse was the hand washing basin.

As well as used kit being cheaper to buy, the maxim 'they don't make them like they used to' sometimes holds true. Some bakers have found certain older bits of equipment to be more reliable, easier to maintain and repair, and better for the job in hand than some newer ones. How many bakers have we seen using Hobart and Artofex mixers that are – in some cases decades – older than they are?

 We started by making two loaves at a time in our Ikea oven at home and most of our equipment was second-hand. For a couple of months we kneaded up to 115 loaves per bake by hand, but this got pretty tiring. We found a 30-quart Hobart spiral mixer on eBay, which had been cleared out of a school. We got rid of the telly and plonked the mixer in our living room until we decided on getting our own premises. We then got most of our steel workbenches from eBay but our oven, bread racks and big mixer came from Belmont Bakery Machinery, because they had been serviced and we needed that peace of mind."

Dan McTiernan, founder of The Handmade Bakery, Slaithwaite

 Another source worth considering is catering auctions, especially if you're lucky enough to know the chap in charge, as we did. A bit of insider knowledge is enormously helpful but if no one else is interested in what you're looking for, you can get some real bargains."

Maggie Rich, Companions Real Bread, Bedford

Potential disadvantages

The possible downsides of used equipment include that it might:

- Not last as long as new.
- Be more prone to breaking down sooner and more often.

- Be less energy efficient, which has financial and environmental implications.
- Lack safety devices (eg interlocking guards and instant brakes) that may now be advisable, or even required by law.

Used equipment that hasn't been reconditioned (or at least checked by a technician) might have developed dangerous faults that are not immediately apparent. You could find that the money you save by buying second-hand quickly gets swallowed up and even overtaken by the cost of repairs. Worse still, using it might lead to a serious accident or injury.

Checklist

Things to consider when buying used equipment include:

- Is the seller an established and reputable dealer?
- If not, is there a chance it's stolen?
- Does the item have an up-to-date electrical safety certificate?
- Does the seller provide any sort of guarantee in lieu of one from the manufacturer?
- What are the implications for insurance cover?
- If it breaks down, will the cost of repair outweigh the saving you made buying it? Are the necessary parts and expertise still available?

If question marks hang over the answers, is it really worth taking the punt?

 Anything controlled by a circuit board must be viewed with caution and the availability and cost of replacements ascertained. A 60-year-old, hand-operated pie moulder is probably as good as – and worth more than – it was when new, whereas a two-year-old prover/retarder with a faulty control panel from an unknown manufacturer might be worthless."

Mike Hampson, Becketts

Energy, carbon and cost reduction

Elephant in the room/bakery time: professional bread making (and industrial loaf fabrication) is energy intensive. This has both financial and environmental costs, so have a look at the whole chain from seed to sandwich and think of things that you could do differently to reduce the energy consumption and carbon footprint of your business.

For example:

- Growing grain: using flour milled from grain grown more locally (therefore reducing emissions from transporting it) and/or using less energy-/carbon-intensive farming methods.
- Milling: grain milled more locally using wind or water power (eg a traditional mill) or at least more energy-efficient methods.
- Dough making: look at how far can you go with doing this by hand, after which find an energy-efficient mixer and process. Look at reducing mixing time.
- Proving: reduce or eliminate refrigerated retardation of dough.
- Baking: installing a more energy-efficient oven, keeping it well maintained, only turning on as far ahead of baking as necessary to get it to the right temperature and turning off or right down between bakes.* Scheduling to ensure full loading.
- Cooling: using ambient, rather than refrigerated, cooling of baked loaves.
- Insulation and heat reclamation: water pipes, walls, ceilings etc should be insulated – and open windows, doors and draughts prevented – to reduce heat loss in colder weather. Heat from the oven exhaust can be reclaimed eg for heating water and/or other parts of the building.
- Selling: is a cargo bike an option for at least some deliveries?
- Surplus and waste: see page 228.
- Maintenance: regular checks and, where necessary, recalibration of equipment ensures it is running at optimum efficiency.

*Not as a room heater, as we've heard of some bakeries doing...

Funding and guidance

Look at what is available to SMEs in your country, or more locally, from government and other organisations. For example, The Carbon Trust in the UK has long offered information and – at times – grants or loans:

» www.carbontrust.com

Green energy suppliers

Shop around to find a supplier that offers energy from renewable sources, ideally carbon neutral ones, such as solar, wind, tidal, wave or geothermal.

People

Despite the name, the Real Bread Campaign isn't just about bread, it's as much about people: the folk who grow and mill the grain, through to those who buy and eat bread made from it. At the centre of this web (or wherever in whatever metaphor you choose) is the baker.

There are many microbakers who remain sole traders. Others find that the popularity of their bread (or original business plans) require them to employ staff members. In some cases, a prospective business owner (or group behind a Community Supported Bakery) might plan to do little to none of the bread making and employ bakers to take care of that side of things, while concentrating on running the business.

Recruitment

Among the most - if not *the* most - important assets of a bakery (or any organisation) are its people. If you become an employer, you need to find the right people for the job, which means people with the right personality and attitude to fit into your team, as well as the right skills and knowledge.

Before you recruit

Before taking on a member of staff for the first time, there are some important steps you need to take to make sure you are fulfilling your legal and moral obligations as an employer from the start.

In the UK you need to:

- Make sure the workplace is a safe place for you to have employees, which includes carrying out health and safety and fire safety assessments.
- Register as an employer and set up 'pay as you earn' (PAYE) with HMRC, then register each new employee.
- Check what your responsibilities are regarding pensions.
- Get employer's liability insurance.
- Check a potential employee's right to work in the UK.
- Be sure that your recruitment process doesn't discriminate against anybody, for example on the basis of age, sex, gender identity, colour, ethnic

background, (dis)ability or religion.

- Research whether you need to carry out Disclosure and Disbarring Service (DBS) checks – if you plan to train or employ vulnerable adults, or work with children (eg running baking classes) for example.
- Agree a contract and compensation (pay and benefits).

Other areas of legislation include working hours, holidays, sickness, maternity, paternity, discipline, grievances, dismissals and redundancies.

Diversity, equality and inclusion

Starting with your non-discriminatory recruitment process, what steps will you take to ensure that the power and profit in your business is distributed fairly? Take care that you don't end up in a situation of having a diverse workforce but with people from disempowered groups or marginalised backgrounds only employed lower down the hierarchy on (perhaps much) lower wages.

Find a step-by-step guide to employing people in the UK at:

  » www.gov.uk/employ-someone

Finding bakers

Although there are various baking schools and certifications in the UK, there isn't a single formal route or qualification to become a baker. The resurgence of Real Bread baking as an aspirational profession is relatively recent in places including the UK and, arguably, has yet to gain the same cachet and popularity as being a chef. This means you might find that there is a limited number of applicants with the necessary experience, knowledge and skills to hit the ground running, especially outside major cities. The challenge isn't just a rural one, though. Barriers to bakers' ability to work in cities include higher property prices/rent rates and general costs of urban living.

In addition to bakers who have learned their skills at another bakery, or as a chef, you may well find that your applicants include self-taught microbakers. Don't be put off hiring them, or at least inviting them for a trial shift. We have heard from a number of bakery owners and head bakers that a person's enthusiasm for learning, working hard and fitting in with the rest of the team is as important as their experience. Some bakery owners have told us that an inexperienced baker with these qualities can sometimes be a better new recruit than one set in ways picked up at other bakeries, who needs 'deprogramming' and retraining.

If you have any doubts at the time of the interview, trust your doubts. However desperate you are for more staff, wait until the right one comes along. Never hire anyone without giving them a trial and then putting them on a probationary period."

Romilla Arber, Honesty Group, Berkshire

Advertising

To improve your chances of getting a decent number of good applicants, it's worth posting a job advert in as many places as possible. In addition to your bakery's own website and social media accounts, options in the UK include websites such as FoodmanJobs, Gumtree, Countertalk and Sustain's own www.rootstowork.org

If you have a shopfront or market stall, you can also try putting up a poster. If you receive unsolicited CVs or enquiries when you're not actively looking for staff, it's worth considering keeping them on file and contacting those people the next time that you are. You can also ask around your Real Bread friends to see if they have any good bakers who are looking to move on, either as a promotion, change of location or simply to gain different experience.

Managing a team

Getting the most out of a team, who in turn benefit from working with you, requires investment of time, money and more. As part of this virtuous circle, the best business owners and managers value and nurture their teams, helping them to develop personally and professionally. A happy and fulfilled employee is more likely to stay with a business, working efficiently to make a greater contribution to its profit and culture.

Relationships

It is useful to build mutually respectful, professional relationships within your team. Morgan Williams, who has managed various bakery teams, suggested: "Assume good intentions, even when something goes wrong; occasionally even the most diligent employee will forget to put the salt in the mix and it is unlikely that a person has deliberately created more work for themselves. Try to foster an environment in which people feel able to come to you with suggestions for change. If they do, try to take their feedback and criticism on board without reacting impulsively or emotionally. In some cases, it might be better to get back to your employee later, rather than giving a less considered answer immediately."

Work on the business not in it. If you attempt to be the baker and run the business you might burn out quickly – you are only human after all. There are lots of excellent people out there who are better at making great bread than you and who want a paid job doing it. Seeing my team thrive and excel beyond my own baking capabilities is a really uplifting and humbling feeling."

George Casey, Haddie & Trilby, Warwickshire

Pay

Beyond any minimum wage that might be legally required in your state or country, consider the benefits of paying staff an enhanced salary, such as the Living Wage in the UK.

 Even though we're a not-for-profit, have limited funds and are not signed up to the scheme, we voluntarily pay the London Living Wage. We're not even in London, but we do it because we want to show our team members that their work is valued."

Simon Cobb, Stoneham Bakehouse, East Sussex

Tips and gratuities

If tipping is the norm for your business (more common if you run a sit-down eatery), you should have a policy on how tips are allocated. Does each member of staff keep their own, or do tips get pooled and divided in a set way, for example through a tronc? We do not advocate UK employers assuming that tips will make up pay packets, though this might be acceptable in other countries where the tipping culture is strong enough to be relied upon. In many countries, tax has to be paid on tips, so check the rules with your national tax/revenue office/department.

Benefits

Small benefits go a long way. Could you provide meals for your employees as part of their package? Consider letting your employees take bread home, whether that's a set amount per shift/week, or limited to helping themselves to any leftovers after closing. In the USA, healthcare might be part of the package. Again, check what, if any, tax implications there might be of employee benefits.

Uniform

If you require employees to wear uniforms and/or company branded items, it seems only right that the company provides them, rather than expecting staff members to pay for them.

Responsibility

As a business owner, you are likely to be more invested in your bakery, both emotionally and financially, than any employee. Allowing someone else to take on responsibility in your business can be quite daunting, especially if you are used to having total control over every aspect of how it runs. Once they have a good idea of how the bakery runs, giving your employees agency to make decisions independently and take a lead in areas can both motivate them to go the extra mile while increasing their job satisfaction.

Put your trust in your staff members. A business is as equally dependent on them as its customers. Within reason allow the staff as much freedom as possible. Keep checking the 'vibe meter' – how's it reading? It's not really about pay, or breaks, or perks, it's about being trusted and given freedom."

Ben Mackinnon, E5 Bakehouse, London

Health and safety

Looking after your own physical health, and that of any employees you have, is essential, not least because of your legal obligations. See page 104 for more.

A successful business needs to be sustainable. This means that staff members, and you, need to be there, *want* to be there and be fit in body and mind to do the job."

Simon Cobb, Stoneham Bakehouse, East Sussex

Training

Every bakery has its own culture and way of doing things. Even the way that Real Bread is made varies from bakery to bakery, and baker to baker. Even if a new member of your team has considerable experience in a respected bakery, it's likely you'll need (or at least want) to give training and guidance on the way you do things in your bakery. In doing this it's worth explaining why you do things the way you do. Often, you'll not realise you have a specific way of cleaning the mixer or folding your dough until you see someone else do it a completely different way. At the same time, watch and listen to your team members as they might bring, or come up with, a great way of doing things that will benefit the business. As the team grows, it can be useful to have a system (and maybe even a bonus scheme) in place to discover and reward innovation and improvement.

> By testing the skills of your bakers, you will be giving them a challenge. By meeting that challenge, they will attain greater job satisfaction."

Peter Cook, Peter Cooks Bread, Herefordshire

Voluntary placements

No matter how informative, books, websites, videos (and even the lavishly tooled *Knead to Know...more*) are, there is no substitute for the hands-on learning experience of working alongside an experienced, professional Real Bread baker.

Some bakeries offer traditional apprenticeships, where the trainee is a paid junior member of staff, perhaps alongside – or as part of – studying for a recognised baking qualification at college. An alternative that can work for some bakeries and trainees is a voluntary placement, during which the volunteer picks up skills and knowledge while proving (increasingly skilled and useful) labour.

> When you are just starting out then any help is always gratefully received. I slipped a disc three weeks into starting to bake. Believe me, volunteers saved us at that point and one of them ended up joining us permanently."

Dan McTiernan, The Handmade Bakery, Slaithwaite

Mutual benefit

A voluntary placement must not exploit either volunteer or bakery owner. It needs to be run as a mutually beneficial arrangement with both parties understanding and agreeing to what they consider a fair exchange. It is important that the owner doesn't treat the arrangement as unpaid labour, or the volunteer sees it as a free baking course.

At first the greater investment will come from the bakery owner. In addition to the value of the skills and knowledge being passed on is the cost of time taken by teaching and supervision, and the cost of slowed production. The presence of a volunteer might reduce productivity even further by taking the workspace of an experienced baker. Over time, however, a willing and well supported volunteer should become a valuable asset to the bakery's team.

Is it appropriate and fair?

Some people consider that it is only appropriate for charities and other not-for-profit organisations, and perhaps community/social enterprises, to take on volunteers. Arguments against a business doing so include:

- However else a person benefits, they should still receive financial compensation for performing tasks that contribute to generating profit for a business.
- A volunteer might deprive someone of a paid job fulfilling that role.
- Volunteering excludes people who are unable to afford to commit time to unpaid work, reinforcing privilege and barriers to social mobility – a concern that extends to the charity and not-for-profit sectors.

Pay and employment law

In the UK, a volunteer doesn't have an employment contract and so isn't covered by employment law. This changes if:

- a contract (whether written, verbal or implied) is created, or
- any consideration (which is the legal term for any form of benefit, monetary or otherwise) is received in return for work.

In either case the law might see the supposed volunteer as an employee who is entitled to some – and perhaps full – workers' rights and pay. What the bakery can choose, however, is to provide (or reimburse reasonable and limited out-of-pocket expenses for) subsistence items: travel to/from the bakery, meals and perhaps accommodation.

In the USA the federal Fair Labor Standards Act prevents private sector employers from taking on volunteers and lays down specific requirements for public sector and non-profit volunteering.

Understanding and respect

In order for a voluntary placement to work, the bakery owner and volunteer must be prepared to make a full commitment to it and both act as professionally as in an employment situation.

To avoid misunderstandings and help the placement to be mutually beneficial (and enjoyable), it is recommended that the baker and volunteer meet up beforehand to discuss and agree upon points such as:

- What the bakery intends to teach the volunteer.
- What the volunteer and the bakery each hope to get out of the experience.
- The member of bakery staff responsible for supervising the volunteer, ideally with regular review meetings.
- Length of the voluntary placement.
- Times and dates of shifts.
- Whether or not the bakery will provide services such as travel to/from the bakery, meals and accommodation, or will reimburse the voluntary apprentice for such out-of-pocket expenses.
- What food hygiene and health-and-safety training the voluntary apprentice has and what more is needed.
- The bakery's other policies and procedures, such as equal opportunities, sustainability and confidentiality.

Volunteer agreement

As a contract is not applicable it's good practice for the bakery to draw up a volunteer agreement covering points such as those above for both parties to sign.

It is also good practice to:

- Provide insurance cover for volunteers.
- Exchange and record contact details of the volunteer, and perhaps next of kin, (ideally mobile phone numbers) in case of any problems.
- Reduce obligations on the part of the volunteer.
- Avoid the use of terms such as job and payment, in favour of tasks and expenses.
- Refer to your expectations for/of a volunteer, rather than obligations.
- Make it clear verbally, and on the written agreement, that neither party intends to create a contract or employment relationship.

Skills exchange

You might choose to organise volunteering through a system such as a LETS (Local Exchange Trading System or Scheme), Community Exchange System or Time Bank.

Old dogs

As every baker does things slightly differently, even the most experienced of bakers can learn new tricks from fellow professionals. We encourage bakery owners to offer and arrange reciprocal staff exchanges or host fellow bakers on one-way visits.

Find out more:
  » UK www.ncvo.org.uk www.volunteeringmatters.org.uk www.gov.uk/government/get-involved/take-part/volunteer
  » Australia www.volunteeringaustralia.org
  » Canada www.volunteer.ca
  » Ireland www.volunteer.ie
  » New Zealand www.volunteeringnz.org.nz
  » USA www.dol.gov/agencies/whd/laws-and-regulations

Bake well

In short, take care of yourself! If you have employees, you have a legal (and moral) duty of care to look after them as well. While much of this is more applicable to bakeries with staff, some is of relevance to sole traders. This chapter was written with the help of baker Morgan Williams.

Body

Being a baker is a physically demanding job, which may well involve heavy lifting and repetitive tasks, all surrounded by a number of hazards. It is easy to mitigate against most of these. Consider what things might be a danger to health and how to prevent or avoid them: eg putting out a wet floor sign when you mop to reduce the risk of slipping, being careful to use proper lifting technique when handling bags of flour or heavy boxes of dough.

Much of this section is pitched at a bakery with employees, but the home-based microbaker should give it a read to be aware of good practice and any legal requirements. Check with your local authority if they offer advice on health and safety at work.

Burns

These are almost an inevitable part of baking. When sticking your arm in a 300°C (or however hot) oven, you need certain bits of PPE (personal protective equipment). Whether using folded tea towels, oven gloves or baker's elbow-length heavy-duty mitts, make sure they're DRY! You should also consider wearing a top made of natural fibres (they don't melt and are better for a sweaty job) with long sleeves. If (when) you burn yourself, current medical advice is to run it under cool water for at least 20 minutes.

Cuts

Holding a razorblade in your fingers to score or slash dough is just asking for trouble. A lame or grignette (see page 28) to hold the blade will reduce the risk of cutting yourself. Between uses store your lame safely, either in a labelled box or on a magnetic holder and remember to dispose of used blades carefully. If you go through a lot, it might be worth getting a sharps box. Don't try to catch that falling bread knife! If (when) you cut yourself, use a blue plaster – it's conspicuously different from any natural foodstuff.

Back strain and injuries

These should not be as common as they are among bakers. Hefting bags of flour, pulling dough out of the mixer and moving weighty boxes around are all potential sources of strain and injury but, again, they are easily avoided.

Rule one: Bend at the knees!

a. Stand close to and in front of what you are going to lift, with your feet at shoulder distance apart.
b. Unless the object is at chest height already, squat down, keeping your back as close to straight and upright as you can.
c. Get a good grip, using handles if they are available, and take the strain, distributing the weight evenly and staying balanced.
d. Stand up slowly and smoothly, using your leg muscles to do the work, keeping your back straight and upright.
e. Walk carefully, making sure you can see where you're going and that you're not going to slip, trip or hit anything.
f. Squat slowly and carefully place the object down.

Other suggestions:

- Follow maximum weightlifting and carrying guidelines. In the UK they are (a non-gender-neutral) 25kg for men and 16kg for women.
- Consider having flour delivered in smaller sacks.
- Think ergonomically – for example having a sink as close as possible to the mixer to reduce the distance you have to carry water, and mixer close to the bench on which you'll weigh and shape the dough.
- Invest in wheeled trollies and dollies to move dough, finished products and equipment around.
- Bulk prove your dough in smaller boxes, which also has the benefit of having a more even temperature throughout and being less likely to tear as you turn it. Take care when pulling dough out of the mixer.

Too often for my liking, I have issues with my back. It is essential that you take care to not lift anything too heavy, to employ good habits when lifting and standing for long periods of time, or when you need to bend down or turn. Sit frequently and go slowly."

Johanna Bottrill, Jo's Loaves, Luton

Skin irritation

Frequent or prolonged exposure to moisture, cleaning products, and even some oils and other natural ingredients can trigger skin conditions on your hands and arms. If you start getting dry, itchy, red or blistered/flaky skin on your hands or arms visit your GP, and make sure you moisturise your hands and arms after every shift. You might need to start wearing gloves for cleaning and other tasks, perhaps even including dough handling.

Dust busting

One of the biggest dangers to your physical health in a bakery is posed by one of bread's essential ingredients: flour. In fact, in the UK it comes under Control of Substances that are Hazardous to Health (COSHH) regulations. It's a problem not limited to employees of loaf fabricators that use flour with added enzymes.

Although baker's lung might sound likesome sort of 19th century affliction, inhalation of flour dust (as well as spices, other powdered ingredients and cleaning products) can still cause serious respiratory problems such as occupational asthma. Thankfully there are simple steps that the bakery owner can and should take to minimise the amount of airborne flour in the bakehouse, and people's exposure to it, for the sake of everyone's health. For example:

Carry out a risk assessment: where, when, why and how much is flour dust likely to become airborne in your baking operations? Who is likely to be exposed to how much of it for how long and how often?

Sling not: perhaps the easiest ways of reducing flour becoming airborne include being careful as you weigh it out and tip it into the mixer; dusting using a sifter instead of throwing flour around like Paul Hollywood; starting mixers on low speeds; and being gentle as you fold up flour bags.

Dust masks: wearing one when performing especially dusty tasks can further reduce the amount of flour you inhale. If you're a bakery owner, or otherwise responsible for the health and safety of other bakers, also make sure to have plenty of dust masks so that everybody working in the bakery is able to protect themselves.

Don't sweep: clean using a vacuum or wet cloth/mop.

Ventilation: In a smaller operation, opening windows and doors might suffice, while larger bakeries might need to install air extraction and filtering systems.

NB In the UK, bakery owners are legally required to "reduce exposure to flour dust as far below the WEL [working exposure level] of 10 mg/m3 as is reasonably practicable". In 2018, a Yorkshire bakery was fined more than £159,000 for failing to take adequate steps to protect its employees from exposure.

Slips, trips and falls

Choose footwear with good grips. Clean up any spills (including dry ingredients) straight away. Put out hazard signs on a wet floor. Remove trip hazards and clearly mark any that cannot be removed. Don't climb an unsupported ladder, reach up or out too far, or clamber up anything that's not designed to be climbed. Take extra care on stairs. Remove or fix loose floor coverings.

Machinery

Equipment comes with safety instructions and guidelines: read and follow them. It also comes with guards and other protective elements: use them. If using old and/or second-hand equipment, you might need to search for instructions or have the kit modified to bring it in line with current safety standards.

Find out more:

Clearly, this is neither a complete list of risks or a full guide to health and safety compliance. You should consult the relevant national (and, if applicable, regional and local) authority for more information on the various risks in a bakery and the legal responsibilities of employers and business owners for health and safety at work. Starting points include:

» UK www.hse.gov.uk/coshh/basics/index.htm www.hse.gov.uk/coshh/industry/baking.htm
» Australia www.safeworkaustralia.gov.au

» Canada www.canada.ca/en/health-canada/services/environmental-workplace-health/occupational-health-safety.html
» Ireland www.hsa.ie
» New Zealand www.employment.govt.nz/workplace-policies/health-and-safety-at-work/ www.worksafe.govt.nz/managing-health-and-safety/managing-risks/what-risk-looks-like-in-your-industry/bakeries/
» USA www.osha.gov

Dig your own soul

Baking for a living typically involves long – sometimes unsociable – hours and perhaps irregular shift patterns. Even as a home-based microbaker you might have very early starts and/or late nights. It also requires a high degree of mental alertness to ensure accuracy, whether you're weighing ingredients, making up orders or serving customers. Designing your production schedule carefully – including breaks for eating, drinking and even going to the toilet – is essential.

 Running a microbakery can be hugely rewarding, stimulating, satisfying and even exciting, but you won't know any of this if you don't have time to reflect, breathe and take it all in."

Ian Waterland, Knead Good Bread, Leicestershire

The risks of overwork and burnout are increased if you're the bakery owner and combining these demands with the stress of running a small business and being responsible for a team. Morgan Williams, a baker who helped research and write this chapter said: "You don't want to be that baker with shot knees, a knackered back, baker's lung, depression and a wrecked marriage, so take care!"

Diet and exercise

It's important not to overlook connections between mental and physical health. The negative effects that long-term physical strain and injury have on your mental wellbeing and vice versa can be huge. Looking after your physical health is a good way to begin looking after your mental health. Regular exercise (not simply the work you do when baking) and having a balanced diet will help you avoid physical injuries and also support your mental wellbeing.

Working hours

Exhaustion or burnout is caused not only by physical overwork, but also by sleeplessness and stress, and it can manifest itself both mentally and physically. One of the ways in which being a baker can significantly affect your health and wellbeing is the effect of how long you work and at what time of day or night. There are ways in which you can try to mitigate the impact of this for yourself and (if applicable) your staff.

As a bakery owner or manager, consider early baking shifts being shorter and later mixing/shaping/cleaning shifts being longer. For example, four ten-hour late shifts instead of five eight-hour shifts in a week gives bakers an extra day off. Avoid split shifts and try to group days off together so people are properly rested. If your bakery is open on Saturday and/or Sunday, make sure to rotate shifts so weekend days and (ideally) full weekends off are shared out. Avoid putting bakers on a later shift without at least a day off in between. Play to people's strengths as much as you can – some people thrive when working late or at night, while others prefer early or mid shifts.

According to UK law, you need to ensure that your staff members have at least 24 hours uninterrupted rest per week, or 48 hours without work every fortnight, and there should be at least 11 hours between the end of one shift and the start of the next. Also:

- Any work between 11pm and 6am is considered night work and anybody working three hours or more between these hours is considered to be a night worker.
- Night workers shouldn't be working more than an average of eight hours in a 24-hour period.
- This average is typically calculated over a 17-week period, but it can be over a longer period of up to 52 weeks if the workers and the employer agree.
- Shifts should be restricted to eight hours (ie the average does not apply) for night workers doing heavy physical work, which might apply to bakers doing frequent/regular lifting of flour sacks, dough etc.

Sleep

Following on from the above is how much (or little) sleep you get, when you sleep, and the quality of sleep. There is evidence that chronic sleep deprivation can have a negative impact on your physical health, such as increasing your chance of heart disease, becoming obese and developing diabetes.

There are ways to reduce the effect of night shifts. Having regular shift patterns and getting into a regular sleep routine can help. Invest in some good blackout curtains (or an eye mask) and earplugs, and avoid caffeine in the six to eight hours or so before you want to go to sleep. Make sure you eat properly during your shift and drink plenty of water. Try to get as much sleep as you can, when you can – anything less than seven hours is going to have a detrimental effect on your health.

The post-bake afternoon power nap is your friend. According to some, an hour and a half is the optimum, because that is how long it takes to complete one sleep cycle. Otherwise you should apparently keep it to 20 minutes or you will wake up during deeper sleep and might feel worse than you did before.

The power of no

The popularity of Real Bread means that you might be tempted to bake more things and in larger amounts, or to take on a mass of wholesale customers, even though this might not be the best thing for you personally.

Before he set up his Knead Good Bread microbakery and mindful baking classes, former Campaign ambassador Ian Waterland was a mental health professional. Here are some of his thoughts:

"Knowing when to say no is far more important than saying yes. If a potential customer does not fit your business model and ethos – the reasons why you are a baker – then they are not your customer. In the early days of running my bakery I said yes to people when I should have said no. The 'success anxiety' was hard to ignore. The result was lower satisfaction and a general feeling that I wasn't doing what I wanted to be doing when I retrained as a Real Bread baker. With hindsight I should have stuck to my guns. Wholesale customers could be particularly challenging with varying demands and unrealistically low price expectations. I no longer supply any of them. If you are baking at full capacity for customers who aren't the right fit, you simply won't have time for ones who are.

The ability to say NO is something which can be difficult to master, especially in a fledgling business when money is tight and work sporadic. My opinion is that for a business to be around in five years, the ability to decline work, which either does not fit your business model or will deny you essential gaps in which to breathe, reflect, sleep and maintain some semblance of family life, is essential. Be in it for the long term.

You might receive a lot of approaches for work, supplying cafés or restaurants, special events and teaching. If the work fits with your ethos and makes sense business-wise, then fine. If not, then my suggestion would be to discuss options to find a solution that works for you and the customer, or just say no."

This is echoed by Adam Pagor, who in 2019 took the leap from running a home-based microbakery to open the Grain and Hearth bakery and café in Whitstable: "My main advice is to start small and build. Remember that you're not running a big bakery with loads of staff and equipment and not to enter any wholesale relationships under that guise."

Adam's tips include:

- It's too easy to work way more hours than you should as you're at home and sometimes it doesn't feel like work. Set yourself working hours. Try to stick to them and find a way of turning off after you've finished for the day. This will help keep you feeling mentally well.
- Avoid offering a six or seven day a week service: it's not sustainable without staff. Make sure you have rest days.
- It's important to set boundaries at the beginning of new wholesale relationships. Always let the customer know what you can do and on what days. Don't accept orders for things you don't make or on days you don't bake.

Louise Williams, who runs BakerLou in Cheshire, sums it up like this: "The life of a baker is busy enough. Don't burn yourself out trying to please everyone."

When do you say stop?

The answers to questions such as 'Can you grow too quickly?' and 'Is there a size limit?' depend on your priorities and the reasons that you are baking Real Bread. If you're in it for the money and your definition of success is centred on generating more profit than the year before, then perhaps the answers to both will be no.

Alternatively, your key drivers might include philanthropy, a creative urge, or your environmental conscience, and you may decide that a slow and steady growth to a level at which you are breaking even or turning only a small profit is the way forward.

Honesty Group founder Romilla Arber said: "Growth means more people, especially in Real Bread production. This can bring extra challenges - HR headaches and so forth. Remember why you started your business. If it was to have to only answer to yourself and your customers, then large growth is not for you."

Back in 2010, The Handmade Bakery co-founder Dan McTiernan wrote: "Yes you can grow too quickly! Don't do it! Burnout is a real risk. There is such a demand for good bread that if you said yes to everyone you would collapse in a heap within six months. Be honest with yourself about what you need (financially, socially, family-wise…) and don't compromise that. We have had requests to supply food service businesses that make sandwiches for British Airways and Marks & Spencer as well as from two supermarket chains and we could have expanded to be at least ten times bigger than we are currently within the first 18 months of baking. If that's what you want, then great, but that was not our goal.

"We set out to provide Real Bread for our local community and to create at least two livings out of it, but already we have gone beyond that. To date, we have created the equivalent of three full-time jobs, spread between nine people, which makes it sustainable for all of us. There was a point, however, at which Johanna and I were doing nearly everything on our own and this was very tiring and mentally and emotionally draining. Now we have others involved, it is much more rewarding and energising.

"We believe in finite growth and are unconcerned that this is swimming against the current capitalist thinking for business. We are happy to have a small thriving bakery that is making enough loaves to make it financially stable without compromising quality of bread and happiness of employees. Beyond that, we are not interested. Any growth for us would then be sideways into other interesting sister projects, such as more education or wheat growing.

"We also have a 'kitchen table' rule with business partners and customers, which is to say that we only work with people we would be happy to invite into our home and share food with round our kitchen table. This has stood us in good stead so far!"

Smells like team spirit

In researching this chapter of the book, the importance of having a team of people who get along with each other was a recurring theme among the bakers with whom we spoke. Many find it vital in being able to enjoy their jobs. As Carmen Facio of E5 Bakehouse put it: "You spend more time with your teammates than you do with your family, so if you don't get on or there is friction and tension it can really affect your happiness."

Morgan Williams said: "Even when your mind is tired from a 3am start and your back is aching from lifting dough boxes, having a co-worker you have a good relationship with turn up at 7am can really lift your spirits."

Being the boss

Key to the culture of a bakery is the personality and actions of the owner. Many of the bakers we contacted cited the attitude of their employer as one of the most important things that keeps them happy in their jobs.

Being involved with the day-to-day work in the bakery, from facing the challenges of changing weather to helping to pull dough out of the mixer, can have an uplifting effect on your team. It can enhance your ability to cultivate a positive, supportive, collaborative environment, and to spot and head off potential issues before they become serious problems. When things do go wrong, being there to help dig the team out of the **** can help a feeling of 'we're all in this together'.

If and when your bakery grows, your role as owner inevitably becomes more managerial. This can be difficult for you and your team members. As the owner of a business with staff members, you should have a trusted deputy or two to be there when you can't, whether that's while you're on an admin day/shift, or taking well-deserved time off. You should be able to entrust them with the authority, ability and confidence to make decisions on your behalf. They can be your eyes and ears, passing information and messages from you to the rest of the team and vice versa.

This isn't a baking book, but...

Some stuff about bread making

Obviously you're pretty darn good at making bread, or you wouldn't be considering running a microbakery business. During and beyond your transition to being a pro, however, there are some things that you might not have known (or needed to know) about. This chapter contains stuff that you might not have come across in domestic baking books, and some not covered by guides for professional bakers.

Ingredients

By adding time – plus your skill and knowledge – it's possible to produce great Real Bread from off-the-shelf ingredients, even ones that are cheap at the checkout. There is, however, truth in the old sow's-ear-silk-purse adage, and there are other good reasons to put a bit more thought into the ingredients you choose to use.

In general, think positive for people and planet. We encourage you to use ingredients produced to higher environmental standards – such as those certified biodynamic or organic. We are concerned about gene editing and other forms of genetic modification and support the work of Sustain member organisation GM Freeze.

Seek out ingredients produced as locally as possible by your fellow small, independent producers. In the case of ingredients that can't be produced anywhere near you, look for Fairtrade certification or other reliable assurance that producers are being paid fairly and otherwise not exploited.

You might find yourself facing a choice – eg between grain grown and processed locally in a 'conventional' system and certified organic flour produced further afield. This can involve weighing up a number of pros and cons, and some of the following notes might help you make your decision.

Flour

As the main ingredient of Real Bread, flour is the most important building block of your loaf. At a global level, wheat is the third most produced grain after maize and rice. Wheat, usually cultivars of the species *Triticum aestivum* – aka common or bread wheat – is used to make the majority of the world's bread, industrial loaf products and other baked goods.

Broadly, there are three factors used to classify wheat:

- Grain hardness – hard, medium or soft.
- Kernel colour – red, amber or white.
- Planting season – winter or spring.

Typically:

- Hard wheat is higher in protein, and produces stronger gluten, than soft.
- Red wheat is higher in protein, and produces stronger gluten, than white. It also tends to have a more pronounced flavour.
- Spring wheat is higher in protein, and produces stronger gluten, than winter.

Hard red spring wheat tends to produce the strongest flour, which is considered by some bakers to be the 'best' for bread making. That said, other factors including growing and storage conditions can have a huge influence on the gluten content and strength.

Categorising wheat by hardness, kernel colour and planting season is seen by some as crude. The nuances of wheat are more subtle, with varieties, soil types, farming practices, crop densities, local climate and more all having an impact on grain quality and its suitability for bread making. What constitutes 'best' also depends on the end results you're aiming for, as well as on other factors, some of which are outlined in this chapter.

Read more:
- » *Wheat for bread and other foods*, by R.J. Peña www.fao.org/3/y4011e/y4011e0w.htm
- » Various discussion threads at www.thefreshloaf.com

Better bred bread

Although the type of flour you use is not a criterion in the Campaign's basic definition of Real Bread, we encourage bakers to consider the various benefits of using flour that is milled in one or more of the following ways:

- By mill stones, rather than steel rollers.
- Using renewable energy (eg wind, water or solar power).

- At 100% (ie wholemeal) or other high extraction rate.
- From non-commodity grain.

You might also choose to explore using freshly milled flour and/or sprouted grain flour.

Local producers

Is there an independent mill in your area? By using its flour you will forge a personal link in the seed-to-sandwich food web, helping to support your local economy and heritage, and minimising the energy used to transport the flour. If it is a traditional wind- or water-powered mill, the energy used in milling will be non-polluting.

As Nick Jones, former chair of The Traditional Cornmillers Guild (TCMG), wrote in the first edition of this book, "For the artisan baker, traditional mills are natural partners, as they produce such a range and variety of flours, providing exactly the local quality and distinction that marks them out from 'run o' the (roller) mill' bakers. Think of flours and breads like wine. Just as every vintage, every vintner and every vineyard has a distinctive quality, so too different mills produce different flours!"

He also noted that traditional mills tend to:

- Provide local employment and volunteering opportunities.
- Preserve traditional crafts and skills.
- Contribute to the tourism economy.
- Offer an invaluable educational resource that might include tours, craft and engineering training, and baking classes.
- Supply a range of flours and cereal products, often milling to individual needs.
- Work closely with nearby farmers and use locally grown grain.

Local supplies and stores of grain are more resilient to short-term supply disruption by factors such as adverse weather conditions, industrial action and fuel shortages.

Organic ingredients

The number and levels of toxic petrochemical herbicides, fungicides and pesticides used in lower input farming methods (such as organic and biodynamic) are lower than in 'conventional' systems. The amount of petrochemical fertilisers used is also lower. Some organic and biodynamic farmers use no agrochemical inputs at all. This results in a lower negative – or even a positive – impact on the health of the soil and surrounding water systems, and reduces or eliminates potentially toxic chemical residues in the food chain.

Many 'conventional' cereal farmers in Britain – and other cool, damp places – even spray their wheat with glyphosate shortly before harvest, not as a herbicide but to help dry the grain ahead of storage. According to a Pesticides Action Network UK report in 2014, Defra found pesticide residues in the majority of UK-produced flour and loaf samples tested, but found no residues in certified organic products. The Defra report for the third quarter of 2019 found residues in 134 out of 137 'bread' samples tested – again all were the result of 'conventional' farming. Yummy.

Stone versus steel

The wheat grain (aka berry) comprises a starchy, white endosperm tipped with an oily and vitamin-rich germ, surrounded by the protein-laden aleurone layer, all protected by a jacket of high-fibre bran. In traditional milling, crushing the whole grains between two horizontal, circular millstones keeps all parts of the grain together and intermixed.

Nick Jones said, the process "is designed to produce wholemeal flours with excellent flavour and nutritional value. Nothing is taken away in the process – whole grain goes in and wholemeal flour comes out, so the flour retains its integrity. The oily, flavoursome, nutritious wheat germ can't be separated out in stone milling, so it gets spread throughout the flour and provides a delicious, characteristic nutty flavour." Even when sifted to remove much of the most fibrous, nutritious and flavoursome parts of the grain, the resulting lighter-coloured flour will still contain some fine particles of these parts.

Most modern mills, instead of stones, use a series of steel rollers that are ruthlessly efficient at systematically shearing, breaking and separating parts of the grain into many fractions or streams. These streams are then recombined in varying combinations and proportions to produce standardised products with consistent baking qualities. In the case of white flour, the result is a powder that's little more than starchy carbohydrate and gluten-producing protein. In an attempt to compensate for some of the lost nutritional value, so-called 'fortification' of flour with a handful of 'token nutrients' by millers is mandatory in Britain and some other countries – see below.

Published in the January 2020 issue of *Trends in Food Science and Technology*, a study on the effects of milling methods on bread making concluded that wholemeal loaves produced with a particular stoneground flour had greater volume. The flour can vary (sometimes greatly) from batch to batch, however, requiring the baker to make recipe and process adjustments for consistency of results, or embrace and enjoy the differences of each unique batch – and encourage customers to do likewise.

Wind and water

A milling company using energy derived from burning stuff might choose to plant trees in an attempt to help 'offset' the carbon dioxide that generates, which is great – it's always nice to see people planting trees. A traditional mill powered by wind or water, meanwhile, has a far smaller carbon footprint problem to address in the first place... and they can still plant trees as well!

Higher extraction rates

The percentage of the de-husked and cleaned wheat berry that makes it into the flour sack is known as the extraction rate. Generally speaking, the higher this percentage, the higher the fibre and micronutrient (vitamins, minerals etc) content and, therefore, the greater its potential contribution to a healthy diet. Higher extraction flours typically have a more pronounced grain flavour. These aren't hard and fast rules, as a partly refined stoneground flour might have a greater micronutritional content and levels of flavour and aroma than a roller-milled flour of higher extraction.

UK law requires that wholemeal flour must be 100% extraction. Roller-milled white bread flour produced in Britain will be around 78-81% extraction and brown flour will fall somewhere in between, usually 80-85% extraction. Extraction rates for sifted stoneground flours can fall outside these ranges. This information is rarely shown on bags of flour for domestic use but a miller or ingredients supplier will be able to tell you what you are getting.

Potential downsides of using high-fibre flours include that they can exacerbate digestive issues (eg Irritable Bowel Syndrome) in some people. They also contain higher levels of phytic acid, which can inhibit the body's ability to absorb certain micronutrients, though longer fermentation using a sourdough starter culture can help to reduce levels of phytic acid, as can sprouting grains - see below.

Landrace and other non-commodity grains

In the UK and the rest of Europe, a landrace is officially defined as "a set of populations or clones of a plant species which are naturally adapted to the environmental conditions of their region." That is to say seeds that have been saved and resown year after year (perhaps for decades or centuries) in the same area and a form of natural selection has taken place. A folksier term for a variety that has been passed down through the generations is 'heirloom'.

With no legal definition, the term 'heritage wheat' is open to interpretation. One view is that the line in the sand should be drawn somewhere in the 1800s. By the end of that century, many farmers – particularly in more industrialised nations – had moved away from saving and sowing long-straw landrace wheats towards buying in single cultivars developed by commercial seed breeders. Others argue that the cut-off should be the introduction of – and hybridisation with – dwarf wheats, coupled with a steep rise in agrochemical use in the wake of World War II.

Typically, landrace and heritage wheats are naturally resilient, having been selected over generations for genetic traits that include the ability to thrive in particular conditions without the input of artificial fertilisers or biocides, on which more modern varieties tend to be heavily dependent. Champions of older wheats also vouch for their greater nutritional value. Some even claim the grains are better tolerated by people who have difficulty stomaching newer ones, though more research is needed before any definitive statements can be made. For now they have to be qualified – some people report that they can eat certain specific older wheats, for example. On a subjective note, heritage grainiacs argue that older wheats have better flavour.

In the UK and the EU, seeds of any given variety/cultivar of a cereal – or other plant – can only be marketed (ie sold, given or otherwise transferred) to be grown as food if it has been registered on a national list of varieties. This process involves the cereal/plant breeder jumping a number of hurdles, including demonstrating that the variety is distinct, uniform and stable (DUS), having it tested (which takes years), keeping records and paying fees. A similar process applies for the listing of a landrace for conservation purposes.

At the time of writing, of around 300 wheats on the UK national list, there was only one conservation variety of wheat (Squareheads Master, dating back to the 1860s) and nothing else that could be considered a heritage variety. The next oldest on the list was Maris Widgeon, first made available around a century later, in 1964.

Brockwell Bake's wheat:gateway gathers together data about hundreds of thousands of wheat lines from many seedbanks/germplasm collections around Europe and beyond.

> » www.wheat-gateway.org.uk

Find out more:
> » www.open-pollinated-seeds.org.uk
> » www.semencespaysannes.org

Ancient wheats

Another term without legal definition, 'ancient grains' are usually understood to include members of the *Triticum* genus that pre-date hexaploid (six sets of chromosomes) common/bread wheat (*T. aestivum*). The first species cultivated, about 10,000 years ago, was einkorn (*T. monococcum*), which was then crossed with wild goat grass (*Aegilops tauschii*) to produce emmer (*T. turgidum subsp. dicoccum*). Another, khorasan (*T. turgidum ssp. turanicum* or *T. turanicum*), is also marketed under the brand name Kamut. Away from wheat, ancient grains include amaranth, buckwheat, millet, quinoa, sorghum and teff.

Spelt (*T. aestivum subsp. spelta* or just *T. spelta*) is generally considered to be an ancient grain, though critics point towards it being a hexaploid species, so suggest it is better categorised with *T. aestivum*. As *T. spelta* is readily crossed with bread wheat, sceptics also question how much spelt flour on the market is actually from hybrids.

Sprouted grains

Given the right conditions, a grain (eg of a cereal, pseudocereal or legume) will sprout a root and shoot. They can be used fresh and whole or mashed into a pulp; or dried and then either soaked before use, or milled into flour.

Biochemical changes within the sprouting grain include enzymes starting to convert some of the starch in the endosperm into simpler carbohydrates, which the plant embryo uses for energy as it starts to grow. This reduction in carbs means that micronutrients account for a higher percentage of the remaining mass. At the same time, the enzyme phytase starts to break down phytic acid, a so-called 'anti-nutrient' found in grains, which inhibits the human body's ability to make use of certain micronutrients.

Sprouting grains can therefore increase levels and availability of the micronutrients they contain, including B vitamins, vitamin C, folate, fibre, magnesium, zinc, and essential amino acids such as lysine. Some people who have digestive and other issues with certain grains report that these problems are reduced, or do not occur, if the grains have been sprouted. As one of our mantras goes, however – much more research is needed on the potential benefits before definitive claims can be made. As with many things, there is no legal definition of sprouted grain, so how it is used in food marketing varies.

Freshly milled vs aged flour

Received wisdom is that aged or matured wheat flour has better loaf making properties than freshly milled flour. Using wheat flour within hours or days of milling (sometimes known as 'green flour') can result in sticky, slack dough that doesn't rise well. When wheat flour is stored in the right conditions for a month or two, oxidation leads to changes that tend to result in a stronger and more elastic gluten matrix, which means greater gas retention capability and potential to produce loaves with greater volume. This 'aged' or 'matured' flour also tends to have a greater capacity for water absorption. It's one of the reasons that some millers started adding all sorts of oxidising agents to their flour to speed up the process.*

Freshly milled flour has many advocates, though. Some small bakeries have installed stone mills to produce at least some of their own flour, while small tabletop versions are growing in popularity among microbakers. An article in the March-April 2018 issue of Cereal Foods World noted: "The motivations for this include enabling a closer connection to the farms where the grain is grown, a perception of better flavour derived from very freshly milled grain, and claims of health benefits for very fresh flour, which may not be supported by evidence." On the last point, unrefined, freshly milled flour does indeed contain more of the grain's fibre and micronutrients than refined flour, but that applies to aged wholemeal, too. Nutrient loss over time might seem plausible, but we have been unable to find any research into the effects of aging flour on its micronutrient content.

Other factors that may contribute to a baker choosing to mill their own flour include avoiding so-called fortificants and other additives, bleaches or other treatment agents – see page 205.

*Though now banned in the UK, the rest of Europe and elsewhere, please keep an eye on ingredients lists for such additives where they are still permitted.

Always read the label

When buying flour, always check the ingredients list to make sure that the mill has not thrown in any preservatives, enzymes, chemical 'improvers' or other additives, or bleached the flour. You might want to go as far as asking the miller to confirm the details – we know of one mill in the UK that adds an enzyme to all but one of its flours without declaring it on labels, under the impression that it can be considered a 'processing aid'. We disagree, as it does not perform a function in the flour itself and so is an additive by any definition and, anyway, we believe that all food producers should declare everything, whether or not the law requires them to.

'Fortification'

Some millers add minerals and synthetic forms of vitamins to flour, which is known as 'fortification'. This seems a misnomer to us as more minerals, vitamins, antioxidants and phytonutrients are removed during the roller milling process than are replaced by these substitutes. As UK governmental reviews in 1981 and 2013 recorded, the effectiveness of this approach is in question. Some of these 'token nutrients' are added in forms that cannot easily be absorbed by the body and, therefore, provide little to no nutritional benefit. The reviews also found that the nutritional status of the vast majority of the UK population is good enough to make supplements unnecessary. We believe that there are better ways of improving poor diets than the blunderbuss approach of mass medication of the nations.

In the UK, The Bread and Flour Regulations 1998 demand that forms of calcium, iron and vitamins B1 and B3 are all added to most British-milled bread-making wheat flours, except wholemeal. This so-called fortification is mandatory and so, while we lobby for better ways of improving public health, rather than saying that Real Bread can only be made in Britain with wholemeal flour, it is the exception to our 'no additives' criterion. A similar exception applies to any flour additive in a country or state where its addition is required by law. If you bake with flour containing a particular 'fortificant' or other additive that is not required by law where you are, what you produce is not be what we call Real Bread. For more information see the additives page of our website.

Bleaching

In Britain, Ireland and the rest of Europe, bleaching flour was banned in the late 1990s, largely due to health concerns. Potassium bromate and azodicarbonimide, for example, have been identified as potentially carcinogenic. Bleaching can also further reduce the micronutritional value of already impoverished white flour.

In countries where bleaching is banned, and to which imports of bleached flour are tiny, the descriptor 'unbleached' is effectively meaningless. There is concern that post-Brexit trade deals and regulatory changes in the future might permit the importation of bleached flour to the UK and/or allow bleaching to resume.

In Australia, Canada, New Zealand, the USA and a number of other countries flour bleaching agents are still permitted. In addition to whitening, different bleaching agents have various effects including weakening or strengthening gluten and increasing the water binding capacity of starch. Where available, bleached flour is primarily used for cakes, biscuits (aka cookies), waffles and wafers, but can also be used in loaf making. Bakers in the rest of the world seem to have no problem creating great products without it.

Separating the wheat from the chaff

Claims we've heard, for which we have not been able to find conclusive evidence include:

- **Roller-milled wholemeal flour isn't 100% of the grain** To produce wholemeal flour, by UK law the separated fractions are recombined in the same proportions found in the original grain.
- **Roller-milled wholemeal flour is less nutritious than stoneground** They are both 100% of the grain.
- **The heat of roller milling destroys more micronutrients than 'gentler' stone milling** Millstones tend to operate at higher temperatures than roller mills and, anyway, baking heats the flour to a higher temperature than either method.

Flour types

Something that even the EU hasn't managed to standardise – let alone the wider international community – is flour classification.

Countries including France, Germany and Italy classify their flour types by ash content. This is calculated by incinerating a sample of flour at a very high temperature under controlled conditions and then weighing the residue. The more ash there is, the more inorganic (eg minerals in the bran) matter there was in the sample, so higher numbers tend to indicate higher extraction darker flours, though extraction rates given here are approximate. Other than the Italian system, protein levels aren't specified.

Extraction	Typical use	France	Germany	Italy*
50%	Cakes, biscuits, pastries	Type 40	Type 405	Tipo 00 (9%)
60-70%		Type 45		
72%	Multi-purpose		Type 550	Tipo 0 (11%)
75%		Type 55		
80%	White bread	Type 65		Tipo 1 (12%)
		Type 80	Type 812	
85%	Brown bread			
88-90%		Type 110		
			Type 1200	Tipo 2 (12%)
		Type 150		
100%	Wholemeal bread		Type 1600	Farina integrale (12%)
			Type 1700**	

*The figure in brackets is the minimum required protein content for grano tenero (soft grain) wheat flour commonly used for baking. A parallel system applies to semola or grano duro (hard grain) wheat flour, more commonly used for pasta.

**AKA vollkorn – wholegrain

Names, names, names

In countries including Australia, Ireland, New Zealand, the UK and the USA, it's more or less left to millers as to how they name their flours. These (non) systems of classification are based on suggested use, sometimes in combination with an indication of extraction rate and/or protein content – eg strong wholemeal bread flour. Here are some common terms used, with approximate protein levels in brackets:

Extraction	Common use	Australia	UK and Ireland	USA
<50%	Cakes	Cake (7-8.5%)		Cake (5-8%)
50%	Pastries	Pastry (8.5-9.5%)		Pastry (7.5-9%)
60-70%	Cakes, biscuits/ cookies, pastries			
72%		All-purpose/ plain (8-11%)	Plain (9-11%)	
75%				All-purpose (10-12%)
72-80%	Bread	Bread/baker's (12-14%)	White bread/ strong (12%+)	
~85%	Varies		Brown (9-11% or 12%+)*	High gluten (14-14.5%)
95%	Bread**			Whole wheat/ straight run (13-14%)
100%		Wholemeal (13-14%)	Wholemeal bread/strong (12%+)	

*Brown flour can be made from hard/high protein or soft/lower protein wheats.

**Figures shown for bread flours. High extraction flours can also be made from soft, low protein wheats.

Another system used – particularly in the USA – by some millers and bakers indicates which part of the wheat berry is in the flour.

- Straight run: all of the cleaned grain (wholemeal/whole wheat).
- Patent: taken from the centre of the endosperm. Short patent is the whitest flour, lowest in protein and micronutrients; long patent is marginally darker. Most flours used for cake and bread making are patents.
- Clear: taken from the aleurone layer and outer part of the endosperm. Darker than patent flours and also higher in micronutrients, fibre, oils and flavour compounds. The high protein content of first clear flour can be used to give extra strength to breads made mainly from rye or other low-gluten flours.

Find out more:
    » www.theartisan.net/flour_classification_of.htm

Finding equivalents

Just as there isn't always a direct translation for a word in another language, it's not always possible to find – or create – an exact match between flours classified in different systems. The idea that you can, for example, mix or 'cut' a high-protein strong/bread flour with plain all-purpose or other lower-protein flour to recreate a particular French one doesn't necessarily hold true. Even if the averaged-out protein level in your mix matches the flour you're trying to copy, different varieties of wheat grown in different conditions and then milled and tested differently will result in flours with very different baking properties.

If you're following a recipe from a different country and can't – or don't want to – use imported flour, chat to a miller about what you're trying to achieve and they should be able to point to the most suitable flour from the mill's range. If your bakery's order is large/regular enough, a mill might even produce bespoke flour for you. Either way, a bit of trial and error (or researching what has worked for other bakers) might be necessary. See also the note on page 227 about using non-commodity flour.

Leavening

This is what makes dough rise. Like lever, the words 'leaven' and 'levain' come from a Latin root meaning 'to raise'. Real Bread can be leavened using a live sourdough starter culture (see page 235), or fresh or dried *Saccharomyces cerevisiae* – commonly known as brewer's or baker's yeast. If using any commercially produced yeast, read the label and avoid brands containing any additives – those that do can't be used to make what we call Real Bread. Yeast can be used to seed a pre-ferment, such as a biga or poolish - see page 220.

Not that they're in widespread use, but other options include residues of *S. cerevisiae* from brewing, wine making or distilling; and salt rising, which relies on gases produced by bacteria including *Clostridium perfringens*.

Chemical leavening

Anything leavened using baking powder/soda, or other chemical raising agent, falls outside our (and Real Bread Ireland's) definition of Real Bread. You can find an essay titled *Keep it for cakes* in the articles section of our website.

Salt

In bread making, salt helps to:

- Slow fermentation, though we don't subscribe to the old school idea of adding more salt to act as a 'brake' - you can slow things down by reducing the amount of leavening and/or reducing the proving temperature.
- Strengthen the gluten network.
- Aid the browning process - bread with lower levels of salt may appear paler, while high levels may cause a reddish 'foxy' bloom to the crust.
- Enhance the product's flavour.
- Act as a natural preservative, delaying the onset of mould growth.

Always check the label of commodity (ie mass-produced cooking or table) salt to ensure that it doesn't contain one or more anti-caking agents - sodium hexacyanoferrate, for example. For socioeconomic (and perhaps environmental) reasons, you might choose to use salt from a smaller, independent producer.

Salt and health

In very small amounts, common salt (sodium chloride) is essential for life and pretty useful in food, too. As the UK's Food Standards Agency (FSA) website states, however: "High salt intakes contribute to high blood pressure, which can increase the risk of heart disease and stroke." With our 'better for you' hat on, therefore, we support the use of lower levels of salt than some industrial loaves might contain and, indeed, some old-school craft bakery recipes call for.

In line with Public Health England's 2024 voluntary salt reduction target for bread (and industrial loaf products) we suggest a maximum salt level of no more than 0.85% (ie 0.85g per 100g) of finished product weight. In terms of baker's percentages (see page 217) to achieve this, the amount of salt will be approximately 1%-1.5% of the flour weight. This depends on several other factors, including the hydration of the dough, whether or not there are other ingredients in the bread such as seeds or fruit, the surface area to volume ratio of the loaf, and for how long and at what temperature it is baked.

NB Though in some cases very slightly lower in sodium, 'natural' (eg sea or rock) salts aren't intrinsically 'healthier' than commercial ones. They might contain minute traces of other minerals but you'd have to consume an unhealthy quantity of salt before you reached anything like a beneficial amount of anything else. Nor are they 'saltier' (if anything, the impurities make them less salty), so you need to use the same amount to get the same results.

You can read more about the health issues related to salt at the Action on Salt website:

> » www.actiononsalt.org.uk

Fats and oils

While not at all necessary in plain doughs, fat or oil added in small amounts can be used to perform a number of functions. These include contributing to tenderness or shortness and moistness, increasing dough extensibility (allowing greater volume) and slowing the stiffening effects of staling. Fats and oils can also contribute flavour, help us to taste other fat-soluble flavour compounds, and assist browning, which generates flavour. In the case of some enriched breads and laminated doughs, the use of a particular type of fat or oil is key to the generally recognised essential characteristics of the product.

Reducing or doing without

Unless oil or fat is essential for a particular bread's characteristics, we suggest that you consider not using them. Higher dough hydration will contribute to tenderness, extensibility and slowing the effects of staling. If you do choose to use some in a plain loaf, Andrew Whitley suggested that to achieve maximum loaf volume, you need no more than 5g of fat per 1kg of flour, perhaps a little more for wholemeal.

Palm oil/fat

When a fat or oil label says 'vegetable' some or all of it might have come from oil palm fruit, about which critics, including Greenpeace, have raised environmental and other ethical concerns. The main issue is that they believe that palm oil certification systems are either not robust or policed well enough to guarantee that no rainforest clearance has been involved. This destroys the natural habitat of wildlife, including some endangered species. The Bank of England, which looked into using palm oil in the production of a new £20 note, also noted: "Forest fires, started to clear land for oil palm, release high levels of carbon dioxide and black carbon into the atmosphere, contributing to climate change." There are also health questions that hang over the type of saturated fats found in palm oil.

Conversely, the BBC has quoted Dr Emma Keller from the World Wide Fund for Nature as saying: "We can produce a lot more palm oil per area of land compared to other oil crops like soybean oil or coconut oil. Palm oil has provided jobs for millions of small farmers, helping them to get out of poverty, earn more money and have a better life for them and their families." The article also notes that: "It is also reported that oil palm trees do not require as many pesticides or fertilisers to be used when growing them."

Animal fats

Subjectively, many people enjoy the taste of butter, lard and other fats of animal origin. Others choose to avoid them on moral grounds (the use of animals for food), based on religious beliefs, for environmental reasons (farming cows has a huge carbon footprint), due to health concerns, following a trend, or steered by a general 'vegetable = good, animal = bad' message currently promoted by many health professionals and through various media outlets in the UK and elsewhere.

Sustain advocates a 'less but better' approach to meat, dairy and other animal products. It is up to you – in conjunction with the needs and wants of your current and potential customers – to decide which, if any, animal fats you use.

Saturated, unsaturated and trans fats

An article published by Harvard Medical School in 2019 suggested: "Avoid the trans fats, limit the saturated fats and replace with essential polyunsaturated fats." Monounsaturated and polyunsaturated fats are essential in building and maintaining the human body. They can help reduce harmful LDL cholesterol and lower triglycerides. Common sources are oils from vegetables, nuts, seeds and fish.

By contrast, a diet high in saturated fat and/or trans fats has been linked to raised levels of blood cholesterol and an increased risk of coronary heart disease. Saturates are found in high levels in animal fats (eg butter and lard) and hydrogenated and partially hydrogenated oils/fats, including some white/vegetable fat/shortening sold to the baking industry, and in ultra-processed spreads that were marketed to us for decades as 'healthier' alternatives to butter... Trans fats are found in butter in small amounts, and in higher levels in hydrogenated and partly-hydrogenated oils/fats – though the latter have been banned in the USA and elsewhere.

Find out more:
   » www.health.harvard.edu/staying-healthy/the-truth-about-fats-bad-and-good

Other ingredients

While other natural ingredients (eg seeds, nuts, cheese, milk, eggs, malt extract, herbs, dried fruits etc.) are not essential for plain bread, we don't exclude them unless they have been processed and additives have been used.

Ingredient suppliers

The flour market in the UK (and some other countries) is dominated by a handful of national and multinational companies, often milling imported commodity wheat. If you have specific questions (eg the cultivar/variety of grain, how it was grown, how it was milled, if a sustainable source of energy was used for milling etc) of any given flour, please check with the miller in question.

Please also check with the mill that they don't add enzymes or throw other non-mandatory additives into the flour or mix you intend to use. Sadly, even some smaller, family-owned independent mills do. By our definition, a loaf made with such a flour or mix is not Real Bread.

Independent mills

Here's a small selection of independently owned mills in the UK that offer regional or national distribution. Most produce a range of flours and some offer a bespoke service for commercial bakers. You can find many more smaller mills in the UK and beyond on our website's Real Bread Map.

- Doves Farm Foods, Berkshire www.dovesfarm.co.uk
- Gilchesters Organics, Northumberland www.gilchesters.com

- Scotland The Bread, Fife www.scotlandthebread.org
- Sharpham Park, Somerset www.sharphampark.com
- Shipton Mill, Gloucestershire www.shipton-mill.com
- N R Stoate & Sons, Dorset www.stoatesflour.co.uk
- Tamarisk Farm, Dorset www.tamariskfarm.co.uk
- Yorkshire Organic Millers, Yorkshire www.yorkshireorganicmillers.co.uk

Finding a local mill

For a truly local loaf, you need a mill as close to the bakery as possible that produces flour from locally grown grain. If you've not found one on the Real Bread Map, here are some other places to look:

- The Traditional Cornmillers Guild www.tcmg.org.uk
- The Society for the Protection of Ancient Buildings: Mills Section www.spab. org.uk/spab-mills/
- UK Flour Millers (FKA National Association of British and Irish Millers or NABIM). Members include both independent millers and the larger companies that dominate the market www.ukflourmillers.org

Non-commodity wheats and local grain networks

Why not seek out, or even help to form, a local grain network? These collectives typically comprise researchers, breeders, farmers, millers, bakers and other people working to establish sustainable and equitable local grain economies. Often they will choose heritage grains, sometimes planted in mixed landrace populations. Criteria for selection may include flavour, nutritional value and suitability for local growing conditions with low to no agrochemical input.

Examples in the UK (some of which were in their infancy as we were editing this edition of the book) include: The South West Grain Network, East Anglian Grain Alliance, Common Grains (Scotland), South East Grain Alliance, Llafur Ni (Our Grains) Network (Wales) and The Yorkshire Grain Alliance. The Britain and Ireland Community Grains Association website has UK maps of local grain groups and stone mills, plus a list of some farms that grow heritage/landrace grains.

» www.bicga.org.uk

The Grown in Totnes Toolkit includes a guide to setting up a grain network and a directory for other groups to add their details.

» www.grownintotnestoolkit.co.uk

There are many grain networks in the USA. In California, for example, they include: North Coast Grain Growers, the California Grain Campaign, the Tehachapi Heritage Grain Project, the Whole Grain Connection and the Mendocino Grain Project.

» www.brockwell-bake.org.uk
» www.growseed.org
» www.grainnetwork.pbworks.com
» www.heritagegraintrust.org
» www.seeds.ca
» www.seedsovereignty.info
» www.semencespaysannes.org

Bakery terms and tips

Professional baking is embroidered with words and phrases that might be unfamiliar to people whose smartphones aren't ingrained with flour. It also involves a wide range of techniques and skills. Here are just some to help you through your journeys in bakerland.

Autolyse

This technique can help if you are using a weaker flour, or find that you're losing strength when you try to increase the hydration of a dough. It involves mixing together flour and water, then leaving it to rest for 20 minutes or more to allow the gluten to start developing. The optimum rest time will vary depending on factors including dough hydration - see below. You then mix in the salt and any other ingredients in the recipe.

Baker's percentages

As you move into the world of professional baking, you will probably start coming across baker's percentages, AKA 'baker's math' in US English. Not every professional baker uses these but advocates say they are useful for:

1. Scaling recipes up or down to a target dough weight.
2. Adjusting proportions of ingredients but keeping the same dough weight.
3. Ignoring weight systems, eg if you're a metric baker following an imperial recipe, or vice versa.

Perhaps confusingly, the percentage of each ingredient is calculated in relation to the weight of the flour, which is always given as 100%. For example:

Ingredient	Weight	Baker's %
White flour	1000	100
Water	750	75
Fresh yeast	20	2
Salt	12	1.2
Total	**1782g**	**178.2%**

If you are using two or more types of flour, their weights add up to your 100% eg:

Ingredient	Weight	Baker's %
White flour	600	60
Wholemeal flour	250	25
Rye flour	150	15
Water	750	75
Fresh yeast	20	2
Salt	12	1.2
Total	**1782g**	**178.2%**

Scaling up or down

One way of calculating the weight you need of each ingredient is:

1. Divide your desired dough weight by the total of the baker's percentages in the recipe.
2. Divide the result by 10 to give you a conversion factor.
3. Multiply the weight of each of the ingredients by this conversion factor.

For example, if you want to produce 20kg the of dough shown above:

1. 20000g ÷ 178.2 = 112.23
2. 112.23 ÷ 10 = conversion factor of 11.223
3. Therefore:

```
600g x 11.223   =   6733.8g white flour
250g x 11.223   =   2805.8g wholemeal flour
150g x 11.223   =   1683.5g rye flour
750g x 11.223   =   8417.3g water
20g x 11.223    =   224.5g yeast
12g x 11.223    =   134.7g salt
```

Total 20000g (ie 20kg)

Adjusting proportions

Baker's percentages come into their own when adjusting proportions of ingredients relative to each other while keeping the final amount of dough the same. For example, you need to increase the hydration, or reduce the salt, but not change the total weight of dough you make. Starting from your desired dough weight (ie how much you want to end up with) you can use baker's percentages to calculate how much of each ingredient you need.

Pre-ferments

When working with a sourdough starter or other pre-ferment (eg biga, poolish etc) double-check how the recipe author has calculated their percentages. They might have divided the 100% between the flour used in the pre-ferment plus the flour in the final dough, or listed the flour for the final dough as 100% and given separate percentages for the pre-ferment ingredients.

Avoiding hard sums

To avoid straining your brain (or calculator finger) you can find free baker's percentage calculators online. Paid-for programs are also available. Alternatively, you can set up a simple spreadsheet (eg in Excel) to do the job for you.

Baking times

Recipes advise baking times but if you make adjustments to the recipe, scaling or method given, you might also have to adjust the baking time and/or temperature.

Baking times largely depend on the weight and type of product, and oven temperature. If an 800g tin loaf baked at 230°C takes around 30 minutes, then a 400g tin loaf might take 22-25 minutes and rolls (eg 100g) 15-18 minutes. An enriched dough will require a lower oven temperature as sugars, fruit, butter, milk and some other ingredients colour and burn easily.

Shape, and whether or not you use a tin, will also affect baking time. For example, even if a baguette weighs 400g, its high surface area to volume ratio might mean the baking time would be less than a 400g tin loaf.

Historically, bakers tapped the bottom of loaves and listened for a hollow sound to check they were fully baked. This might work for the trained ear but, to be sure, professional bakers often use a probe thermometer to check several loaves in a batch. As a guide, the internal temperature for most types of bread should be 90-100°C. If not, put the loaves straight back in, perhaps at a slightly lower temperature to prevent burning if well-browned already.

Deck ovens allow you to control the heat from both the top and the sole of the oven. The temperature controls vary from model to model. Some also have a control to increase the temperature of elements at the front of the oven to compensate for heat lost when opening the door when loading, checking and unloading loaves.

You might find that you get different results when baking at the same temperature setting even when using supposedly identical ovens. Domestic oven and professional ovens alike might have hot spots or develop 'personalities' as they get older. A bit of getting to know your oven is to be expected but you might want to invest in a hand-held laser thermometer and have a word with your oven supplier if there's significant discrepancy between the reading and what the dial says.

Basic methods of bread making

Most bread making techniques around the world fall into one of a handful of basic broad categories:

Straight yeasted dough

All of the flour, yeast, water and salt (plus any other ingredients) are mixed together, bulk fermented, divided and shaped, proved (then perhaps reshaped and proved again), and baked in one continuous process. You might include an autolyse stage (see above) and/or one or more of the proofs may be slowed by retarding – see below.

Sponge-and-dough

A pre-ferment (known by names such as sponge, biga or poolish) consisting of flour, water and baker's yeast is fermented for a number of hours (often overnight) before being mixed with the rest of the ingredients (which might or might not include more yeast) for the final dough. Such doughs can be started with very small amounts of yeast because there is time during the sponge stage for it to multiply. By-products of fermentation in the sponge, including organic acids, will have a strengthening effect on the gluten in the final dough, and can contribute to more complex flavours and aromas.

A portion of dough from one bake can be kept and used to contribute extra flavour, a certain amount of gluten strengthening and some leavening to a new dough. French bakers call this pâte fermentée, while the more prosaic English name is old dough. Some bakers do not class old dough as a pre-ferment as it contributes relatively little leavening to the final dough.

Slow fermentation brings with it a whole new level of flavour."

Peter Cook, Peter Cooks Bread, Herefordshire

Sourdough

Sourdough is a name for a mixture (dough or batter) of water and flour, which naturally contains populations of yeasts and lactic acid bacteria that the baker nurtures into a thriving culture. It is often also used as shorthand for a bread made using such a culture. After the initial nurturing of a starter (which may take up to a week) the sourdough process usually involves three stages:

1. The starter is 'refreshed' by adding more than its weight in flour and water.
2. The refreshed starter is fermented, typically for 12-24 hours, to make a production starter or leaven.
3. Most of the production starter/leaven is used to make the final dough. The remainder is conserved to become the starter for the next batch of bread.

The final dough may contain anywhere from 10-60% sourdough starter by weight, reflecting the relatively lower yeast concentration and gas production compared to baker's yeast.

Read more about sourdough on page 231.

Enriched doughs

These have natural ingredients added at levels that significantly alter the dough structure and behaviour, as well as the eating experience. The principal addition(s) might be lipid (such as olive oil, butter or lard), sugar (which might be in the form of honey or other syrup) or eggs. Nuts, seeds, fruits, cheese, herbs and spices might also be added. Enriched doughs may be leavened with any of the methods above.

These extra ingredients can interfere with gluten formation. You might find you get better results if you make a plain dough and then mix in fat or oil after the gluten has developed. In high enough concentration, sugars can inhibit yeast activity and you might need to use osmotolerant yeast to get the desired volume in some sweet doughs.

Laminated doughs

Layers of cold fat (eg butter, lard or shortening) are folded between layers of dough so that both the expansion of the fat during baking and the aeration provided by the yeast in the dough contribute to creating a very open and flaky texture. Typical examples are croissants and Danish pastries. The trick is to keep everything very cold, which might involve putting the dough into a fridge before rolling and folding again. There are tens or hundreds of layers, so if you make large amounts of laminated dough products, investigate buying a machine to help do the job.

Dough temperature

Home bakers rarely need to worry about dough temperature control but the larger your production gets, the more important that scheduling – and therefore knowing and controlling your dough temperature – becomes. In the professional bakery, a batch of dough must be ready to bake at the time the oven is available – loaves ready too soon can cause a backlog and over-proved dough; while loaves not ready soon enough will result in under-proved dough or an empty oven, which is a waste of time, energy and money.

Optimum dough temperature when using baker's yeast is around 27°C. Assuming the room temperature is around 22-27°C, one way to work out how to get dough to 27°C is by measuring the flour temperature (ft) and then adjusting the water temperature (wt) using this formula: $(2 \times 27) - ft = wt$.

If the flour temperature is 20°C then: $2 \times 27 = 54$, then $54 - 20 = 34$ ie the water temperature needs to be 34°C

As well as the temperature of other ingredients (such as the yeast, any pre-ferment, fat or other additions) a major factor to be taken into consideration for larger scale production is heat generated by friction during mixing – see equipment on page 167.

All that said...

 I don't take temperatures. That just comes from experience of our bakery's conditions. It really is an art that has to be mastered. That's why they call good bakers Master Bakers, I guess. Each baker has to adapt recipes to the conditions of their bakery and the equipment that is available."

Peter Cook, Peter Cooks Bread, Herefordshire

In sourdough, temperature not only has a bearing on proving time but also on the activity of the yeasts and bacteria and therefore the acidity and flavour of the bread. See page 239 for more.

Gelatinisation

In the presence of boiling water, crystalline starch granules in wheat flour rapidly absorb water and become a gel. It's what happens on the surface of bagel dough when you boil them and, to some extent, dough in a steam-injected oven. It also happens inside the dough as it bakes. Mixing flour and boiling water, or even boiling the two together, greatly increases the gelatinisation. The process diverts some of the water from gluten formation, resulting in a softer, more tender crumb structure. It can also help delay staling. It is becoming increasingly widely known under its Japanese and Chinese names of yudane and tangzhong, respectively.

Hydration

This is based on the baker's percentage (see above) of water to flour. For example, a dough with 500g of flour and 300g of water is said to be at 75% hydration. If you are using a sourdough starter or other water-based liquid (not oil) in a recipe, such as milk, you will need to take that into account as well. See the section on baker's percentages for details.

Higher hydration generally allows dough to stretch more and so can result in a more open crumb structure. It can also help bread to stay moister for longer and so delay the effects of staling. A lower hydration works well when you're aiming for a tighter, more even crumb structure – a tin sandwich loaf, or bagel, for example.

Proving, rising or fermentation?

In France the time between mixing and dividing/scaling the dough is called le pointage. If the dough is pre-shaped, left to relax and then shaped again, this stage is called la détente. The period from shaping/moulding to baking is l'apprêt.

In Britain, there isn't complete consensus on what word is used for which stage. Each baker has their own preference as to when (and if) to say proof/prove, ferment(ation) or rise/rising. The period from all ingredients being mixed until the dough is divided ready for shaping is typically called the bulk proof or bulk fermentation, though some bakers call this the first proof. Once the dough is shaped for the last time it is left for what is (usually) known as the final proof. Then there's the transatlantic discussion about whether the past tense should be proved or proofed...

Retarding

This is deliberately slowing fermentation by keeping the dough at a temperature below the optimum for yeast metabolism. The longer proving time allows for extra flavour development and has an effect on other characteristics of the bread. Cold dough is less elastic and, if put straight into the oven, will burst rather dramatically. Some people find 'ears' (or 'eyelashes' if they darken) on the edges of slashes attractive, while others think these sometimes razor-sharp, sticky-out bits are just annoying.

A home-based baker may use a fridge or very cool room. A professional bakery can install a retarder or a purpose-built refrigerated room, in and out of which racks of shaped loaves can be wheeled. Prover-retarders, which allow temperatures to be raised as well as lowered are also available. The costs – financial and environmental – of installing and running a prover-retarder, or walk-in fridge, should be considered – see below.

Control

Retarding gives you more control over when your dough is ready to be baked. This is an important aspect of production that should be considered, particularly in a professional bakery. Early mornings are hard, but night shifts are harder. If you are baking with the intention of having loaves ready for customers early in the morning, instead of having to mix, prove, shape, prove again and then bake in one long process through the night, you can do everything up to shaping the day before, then bang the shaped dough into the fridge/retarder overnight ready to bake early the next day.

If you are moving from an ambient process to one involving retarding in order for the proving time to fit into a particular time schedule, the other two main factors that you need to consider and adjust relative to each other are:

- **Leaven/levain or yeast** If you were making short process doughs using a relatively high level of leavening you might have to reduce the amount. If you had a longer process with less leavening, you might need to increase it.

- **Temperature** At 2-4°C, fermentation slows right down, but a fridge full of dough will take some time to drop to this temperature (especially if the ambient, water, flour and therefore dough temperatures are a lot higher) and so there will be a few hours where the dough is fermenting more rapidly and you will have a shorter proof. On less busy days with fewer loaves in the fridge, the dough will cool down more quickly and so you might have to use slightly more leavening. Of course, you can/should be able to control the retarder temperature and so not have to adjust the amount of leavening or proving time.

It is easier to control the results if you do a more or less full bulk fermentation at ambient temperature, shape this very active dough and then retard the fermentation to a crawl at around 3-5°C. If you are putting less active dough (eg made using less leavening or after a shorter bulk fermentation) into a relatively warmer (6-8°C) retarder and allowing more fermentation to happen in the final proof, you have less control over the process and are more likely to arrive in the morning to find the dough is under or overproved.

Calculations

It is hard to give hard and fast rules as there are so many variables and it's almost impossible to replicate processes exactly from bakery to bakery. Every formula changes how the dough needs to be treated and even the difference in room temperature from one place to another, and from day to day, will have a dramatic effect on the dough. While some baking manuals give formulae of how to adjust the amount of baker's yeast, temperature and proving time relative to one another (and a spreadsheet or app can do the sums for you), in reality experimentation is how you'll find what works for you. Start with your standard formula and process, then adjust one of the three factors at a time until you get a balance that's right for you.

Cash and carbon

Retarding gives a baker more control but before rushing out to buy a swanky new bit of kit, consider the costs, both financial and environmental. The price of buying, powering, maintaining/repairing and eventually replacing a retarder is considerable. The energy required each year to chill tons of dough down by X degrees will add to your bakery's (already pretty large) carbon footprint. Might you instead be able to work out methods and a schedule without one that work for your business, staff and customers?

George Casey, founder of Haddie & Trilby in Leamington Spa, Warwickshire, has found that: "Retarders are expensive, can be complicated to set up and use, and prone to failure. A good gastro fridge or cold room is cheaper, much more reliable, and simple to get to know how your dough behaves in it. Avoid cheap fridges by unknown brands. A second-hand Foster will outlive a cheap internet deal, the build quality on which can be shockingly bad. A cold room is much more efficient on time and space. If you have room, please go for it, you won't regret it. A common baker's gripe is running out of fridge space. Whatever you think you need, you should probably double or triple it."

Scaling

This is the common bakery term for weighing dough. You should always scale dough, not only to ensure even baking of everything in a batch, but also to ensure your loaves end up at the weight you advertise.

The amount of moisture dough loses during baking (and therefore final weight) will depend on baking time, temperature and the ratio between exposed surface area and volume: a kilo of dough might lose more moisture if made into baguettes or small rolls than if kept whole, and a tin loaf might lose less than a boule of the same weight. Other important factors include flour type, dough hydration, other additions and bread making method.

To help start you off, here are some *approximate* scaling weights.

Product and weight	Approximate scaling/dough weight
100g burger bun/sandwich roll	110-120g
400g loaf	480g
800g loaf	950g

You will need to experiment with dough weight (and check average weights of each cooled batch) to ensure that each of your products ends up being sold at the advertised weight. See page 110 for legal aspects of bread weights and labelling.

Shaping

Shaping, or moulding, is the process of manipulating the dough to build up tension in its outer surface that will help control the rising and result in the finished loaf having the desired form. The best way to learn is by working alongside an experienced baker, so that you can watch their actions in 3D, copy them and feel what the dough is doing. They will also be able to put you straight if you've not quite got it right.

Without having a baker to hand, the second-best option is to watch video clips to see the different techniques bakers use for different loaf shapes. Ask your internet search engine for help on this, using terms such as 'bread shaping', 'loaf shaping', or the word 'shaping' paired with the type of loaf you are trying to make.

Using non-commodity flour

If you choose to step away from off-the-shelf bread flour, you have two options:

1. Cutting your coat according to your cloth – make the bread the flour wants you to make.
2. Mixing in a percentage of commercial bread flour.

If choosing the former, take full advantage of the marketing opportunity this gives you – a loaf that is special – or even unique – to your bakery. As miller Nick Jones notes: "English wheat, for example, is generally softer and tastier than imported wheat, but can produce a dense, less risen loaf. Once people have tasted the difference, they tend to be hooked, and are encouraged to bake their own. [Traditional mills'] flours can help to give the small artisan baker an edge and a niche in the highly competitive bread market, where very often the only way to compete with the low-cost, high-volume supermarket offers is to concentrate on something different and special."

To find out what bread a flour is suited to making, try experimenting with: hydration level; leavening (sourdough vs baker's yeast); method (eg sponge and dough, rather than straight dough); fermentation time and temperature; autolyse and/or folding to increase gluten strength; size and shape/form of the bread.

No Loaf Lost

We encourage all bakeries to reduce not only the amount of food they send to landfill (eg by donating leftover loaves to a local charity) but also reduce the surplus they generate in the first place. By reducing your surplus you stand to:

- **Save** money on the ingredients, energy and staff time that go into unsold loaves.
- **Reduce** waste disposal costs.
- **Improve** your environmental impact and reputation for responsibility.

As UK charity WRAP (The Waste and Resources Action Programme) notes in the guide, *Your Business Is Food*: "It's not only food that's thrown away, but the money spent on ingredients, packaging, energy, water and labour to manufacture it. These costs can be anywhere between 5-20 times the cost of disposal."

Minimising food surplus and waste

Our *No Loaf Lost* guide is available to download from our website. It is divided into five sections:

1. Reasons to slice surplus.
2. How to identify when, where and why surplus arises in your bakery.
3. Tips on how to reduce the surplus you create; how to minimise mismatches between production and sales.
4. Involving and communicating with customers and staff on your surplus slicing mission.
5. What to do with any surplus you still produce so that it doesn't go to waste.

Surplus and waste reduction tactics outlined in the guide include:

- Encouraging advance ordering.
- Limiting loaf types.
- Checking external factors, such as holidays, road closures and the weather forecast.
- Keeping shelves attractive without baking extra.
- Using signage to create urgency to buy.
- Suggesting alternatives to sold-out loaves.
- Involving customers as zero waste heroes.
- Weighing (or count) and record your surplus and waste.
- Identifying what's wasted, when, where and why. Looking for patterns.
- Setting reduction targets and incentives.
- Adjusting production according to (better) forecast demand.

We encourage small bakery owners to sign the No Loaf Lost Pledge to take steps to minimise surplus and waste and to promote this important work to customers and other people.

Courses and training

Since the first edition of this book, it seems that some progress has been made in the content of professional courses run by baking colleges and other higher and further education institutions in the UK. It appears that they are still predominantly biased towards additive-assisted loaf fabrication in factories, supermarkets and even some 'craft' operations, though. The teaching of Real Bread skills and knowledge generally seems to remain limited to a small fraction of course time.

The following is just a small selection of schools in the UK that offer professional bakery classes/courses and, in some cases, in running a Real Bread (micro) bakery business. Some offer professional consultancy, as do some of the larger, independent mills.

» **The Artisan Bakery School**, Devon www.theartisanbakeryschool.com
» **The Bertinet Kitchen**, Bath www.thebertinetkitchen.com
» **Bread Angels**, various locations www.breadangels.com
» **Brook Food Processing Equipment**, Somerset www.brookfood.co.uk/bakery-school
» **One Mile Bakery**, Cardiff www.onemilebakery.com
» **Panary**, Shaftesbury, Devon www.panary.co.uk
» **The School of Artisan Food**, Welbeck, Nottinghamshire www.schoolofartisanfood.org

Two that deserve specific mention are Bread Angels and The School of Artisan Food. The first is a large network of microbakers who run classes to pass on their baking skills and business experience. The latter runs its own artisan bakery diploma course, as well as a Foundation Degree in Science (FdSc) in artisan food production with Nottingham Trent University. One Mile Bakery also provides training and support for its microbakery franchisees.

You can find details of many more baking schools on our website's Real Bread Map, and date-specific classes on our events calendar.

Country Rye
Sourdough
1kg - £4.80
720g - £4.10
450g - £2.80
Stick (380g) - £2.20

Sourdough

There's a lot of myth, mystery and misunderstanding (in some cases on both sides of the bakery counter) surrounding sourdough bread, so here's a chapter to help sift *proven fact* from evidence and opinion.

What is sourdough bread?

Genuine sourdough bread is leavened using only a culture of yeasts and (to use yoghurt marketer speak) 'friendly' lactic acid bacteria (LAB). Yeasts and bacteria are present all around us – for example in the air, soil and water. Those well suited to bread production are found living happily and harmoniously in relatively high populations on the surface of cereal grains, such as wheat and rye.

By grinding the grains into flour and providing a suitable environment (see page 235), populations of these microorganisms can be increased to thrive and co-exist in balanced, symbiotic relationships. Eventually there will be enough yeast cells giving off carbon dioxide as a by-product of their metabolic process to make dough rise. The enzymes and other by-products they generate will have a beneficial effect on the flavour, texture and aroma of the baked bread.

At the same time, the number of LAB will increase, typically outnumbering the yeast cells by around a hundred to one. The interaction of these LAB and the products of their respiration (including lactic and acetic acids) also contributes to the taste, flavour, texture and aroma of the bread. Just as with fruit or cheese, it takes time for dough to ripen. Leaving it to ferment for longer increases levels of taste (acid, umami), flavour and aromatic compounds.

Is sourdough 'better' than other bread?

Maybe.

Unless someone has an allergy or intolerance to baker's yeast, there is nothing wrong with it. A skilled baker can make great Real Bread with baker's yeast. A growing number of studies, however, collectively suggest that making bread using a *genuine* sourdough process *might* have greater nutritional and other health benefits.

Over many hours of slow fermentation, LAB produce lactic and acetic acids (and other compounds) that research suggests *might* perform a number of useful tasks, such as:

- Reducing the levels of phytic acid. This is the main form in which plants (especially seeds and pulses) store phosphorus, but it combines with certain minerals including calcium, zinc, magnesium and, notably, iron in a way that makes the human body less able to absorb and make use of them.
- A lowering of the glycaemic index (GI) of bread, which has positive implications for managing conditions including diabetes and obesity.
- A natural preservative effect, delaying staling and inhibiting mould growth.
- Improving the nutritional properties of starch.
- Free amino acids and gamma amino butyric acid (GABA), products of lactic acid bacteria, might increase a sourdough bread's nutritional value.
- Reducing (but not eliminating) the production of acrylamide, a potential carcinogen that is generated in small amounts when starchy foods (such as potatoes and dough) are cooked at temperatures above 120°C. For acrylamide reduction regulation and guidance see page 109.
- Reduction in the gliadin fractions (components of gluten) responsible for triggering the coeliac response and other negative reactions to gluten that some people experience. **NB** This does not make sourdough bread gluten-free or even meaningfully lower in gluten.

Additionally, some people report that they can enjoy eating genuine sourdough, while they find other types of bread and/or industrial loaf products hard to stomach. We publish information and links on our website.

However...

Evidence is not proof and belief is not fact

Whatever you have heard, read or experienced personally, *none* of the above has been proven as general fact. We call for more research to be done on the potentially beneficial effects of sourdough fermentation in order to prove (or disprove) what a raft of relatively small studies have concluded, and to get a better understanding of personal experiences that some people report.

In the meantime, please see page 118 for notes on legal aspects of making claims such as 'more digestible', 'gut friendly' or 'lower in gluten'.

Sourdough bread is not yeast free

If you're marketing sourdough bread as 'made without yeast', 'yeast free' or similar, please stop! It's not in keeping with our value of honest marketing and could breach trading/marketing regulations where you are. Possible alternatives include 'made without baker's yeast', and 'made using naturally-occurring yeasts'.

A sourdough culture will always contain one or more species of yeast. In some cases these yeasts might include the same species (*Saccharomyces cerevisiae*) that is sold as baker's and brewer's yeast, though it is likely to be genetically different to any commercially selected strain.

Concentrations of yeast in a genuine sourdough may well be lower than in bread made with commercial yeast. Yeast cells die at around 60°C and the internal temperature of bread should reach at least 90°C during baking. Some people might still have adverse reactions even to small amounts of dead yeast cells and by-products, though.

The '100-year-old' starter

Is a starter adopted from a baker elsewhere the same as it was under their care? Is one you started yourself the same as it was a few years ago? Possibly not. Studies have found that the populations of yeast and bacteria in sourdough cultures evolve. The flour used in refreshment introduces new yeasts and bacteria each time, while different hydration levels, starter temperature and feeding schedules all influence which populations become dominant.

Over time, these comings and goings can result in a once dominant/majority group gradually dwindling and another slowly 'moving in'. It's a bit like any human community, or the old gag: "This is the axe used to behead Queen Mary. Of course the wooden handle rotted, so that was replaced. Then the head rusted, so we put on a new one. But otherwise, it's the same axe."

None of this takes away from the heritage of your sourdough as a story of human relationships, though. How, where and when you came to become a starter's custodian; from whom you obtained it; that person's tale of how she/he became a custodian; and so on back through time help to make you and the people who eat your loaves members of a cultural network. Even if you began your starter yourself, the story you have to tell is a unique one.

Coeliac disease, food allergy and food intolerance

Some people have genuine medical conditions that cause them to have adverse reactions to certain foods.

Individual triggers and responses vary. Some people cannot eat any cereal containing gliadin (a prolamin protein that combines with glutenin to form gluten), while others have problems with modern wheat (*Triticum aestivum*) but not with spelt (*T. aestivum var. spelta*) or other older members of the wheat family. Some people have trouble with avenin, secalin or hordein – prolamins found in oats, rye and barley, respectively.

Coeliac disease is not a food allergy or intolerance: it is an autoimmune disease that is triggered by the omega-5 gliadin proteins found in cereals including wheat (spelt is a type of wheat), barley and rye. Some coeliac sufferers cannot eat oats, either. In common with other autoimmune diseases (including rheumatoid arthritis) this causes the body to attack itself. In the case of coeliac disease, the immune system produces antibodies that attack the lining of the digestive system, sometimes resulting in perforation of the stomach or intestines. The Coeliac Society estimates that the disease affects around 1 in 100 people in Britain.

An allergy is a condition that causes the body mistakenly to recognise a substance – such as gluten – as toxic and produce histamine in defence. The body then reacts to the histamine in any number of ways, which can include rashes and breathing difficulty. At an extreme level, a person's histamine response is so great it causes the body to go into anaphylactic shock, which in a minority of cases may even result in death.

Food intolerance is a sensitivity that can't be diagnosed by a standard allergy test. The causes are various, including the body not producing an enzyme that is necessary for breaking down a certain foodstuff or part of one; a toxic compound in the food; a pharmacologically active compound (eg caffeine) to which some people are sensitive; or interaction with compounds in the food and drugs that a person is on. Symptoms of a food intolerance could include uncomfortable indigestion and/or excessive gas production, leading to a bloated feeling.

Some symptoms are common to all three types of condition, and also to other totally different conditions and illnesses.

Say no to sourfaux

Any potential benefits of sourdough bread, such as those outlined above, rely on long fermentation in the presence of LAB. Speeding up the process, or removing live LAB from the equation altogether, reduces or eliminates the possibility of the necessary biochemical changes taking place.

The Real Bread Campaign believes that to be named or marketed using the word sourdough, bread (by the Campaign's 'no additives' definition) must be:

- Leavened only using a live sourdough culture, without the addition of baker's yeast or other raising agents, eg baking powder.
- Made without using other souring agents such as vinegar, yoghurt, or inert sourdough powder/concentrate.

More importantly, since 2009 the Campaign has lobbied the UK government for an Honest Crust Act of improved loaf labelling and marketing legislation. This includes a call for the criteria above to be in the basis of a legal definition of the word sourdough.

In the meantime, Campaign co-founder Andrew Whitley coined the term pseudough, and in 2015 Campaign coordinator Chris Young came up with sourfaux, for products marketed as sourdough that fail to meet these simple criteria.

A starter culture can be used in combination with baker's yeast to make Real Bread (it can improve the flavour, aroma and texture) in which case you should include it on your ingredients list for customers to see. Please, *please* don't use the word sourdough in the name or marketing of such loaves, though!

Simple sourdough starter and care guide

You might well have a sourdough starter already, but in case not, here's a simple guide to nurturing one. Forget daft instructions (such as running around with a bowl to 'catch' wild yeasts) or using more than two ingredients - see below. The following is all you need to produce a 100% hydration/liquid starter.

Rye grains seem to host very large microbe populations and, as those critters live on the outside of the grain, your chances improve when using wholemeal flour. It also seems to make sense to use organic flour as the crop won't have been sprayed with fungicides.

Days one to five (ish)

30g rye flour per day

30g water (at about 20°C) per day

On each of the first five or so days, pop equal amounts of flour and water into your container, mix, close and leave at room temperature (again about 20°C) for 24 hours. For the first few days, the mixture might seem lifeless and could smell vinegary or even a bit iffy. Don't worry about this as it should soon start bubbling and the smell will develop into something yeasty and maybe even floral.

This process usually takes about four to seven days but can vary – you might need to keep repeating the flour and water addition (refreshment) for a few more days.

Day six (ish)

Once your starter is bubbling up nicely, you can bulk it up to a quantity needed for your level of production by refreshing with the appropriate weights of flour and water. Feel free to experiment with different ratios of flour to water in your refreshments: a looser starter will ferment more quickly than a stiff one; refreshing more often or adding a lot of flour and water will dilute the taste and acidity.

A large plastic container (sterilised before use) with a lid that provides an airtight seal, but that will pop open if gas production causes pressure to build up, is ideal for storage. Leaving it open, or with a loose/perforated cover, can allow mould and other unwanted organisms in and (if left long enough) allow the starter to dry out.

Wheat starter

Though you can use the rye starter for wheat breads, you might prefer to convert it by replacing the rye in refreshments with wheat flour (white or wholemeal) until it is all wheat. Alternatively, you can start the process above using wheat flour from the word go. Whether you keep a rye, white wheat and wholemeal wheat starter all on the go, or just one, is up to you.

Unnecessary extras

As above, all you need to create and nurture a sourdough starter culture is flour and water. Anything else is, therefore, unnecessary by definition. Here are some suggestions you might have seen, along with thoughts behind them:

- **Grapes, raisins, sultanas etc** Vine fruits often have powdery blooms of yeasts and bacteria on their skins but they aren't necessarily the most suited to making bread.
- **Rhubarb** Acid in the stalks might help to deter pathogenic ('bad') microorganisms and create an environment favoured by lactic acid bacteria.
- **Hops** Also has anti-bacterial properties.
- **Live yoghurt** Acidic and contains live lactic acid bacteria, though not necessarily the types most suitable for producing bread.
- **Mashed potato** A source of starch as food for yeast and bacteria, but flour has more than enough of that.
- **Sugars** Can give the microorganisms an initial 'rush' but, unless you're trying to nurture an osmotolerant starter for sweet, enriched doughs, there's no benefit.
- **Honey** As above for its sugar content. Plus, it's an expensive form of sugar. Unpasteurised honey might also contain yeasts and bacteria but not necessarily the most suited to making bread.
- **Baker's yeast** Makes dough rise but is not an ingredient in a *genuine* sourdough bread or starter.

If any of these work for you, fine – but we reckon don't bother. Just stick to flour and water.

Caring for your starter

A starter is a living thing (well, technically, billions of living things) so get to know it. The acidity, flavour, aromas and speed at which starters work varies, so learn what's normal for yours. Yes, this might sound a bit like a pet or child and in January 2009, Twitter user Louise O'Connor posted: "a sourdough starter is a tamagotchi for people in their 30s". Whether or not you give your starter a name is up to you.

When moving from hobbyist to professional baker, maintaining consistency in your feeding schedules and how you store your starter becomes more important to reduce the variables you will need to adjust for when bread making to maintain consistent quality of your bread.

Storing a sourdough between uses

If you are using a sourdough every day, it can be left at ambient (room) temperature between uses, except if this is likely to be 30°C (eg in hot weather or a hot bakery) which may cause it to become overripe. Over ripeness results in an exhaustion of fermentable sugars and excessive production of acid, both of which can inhibit yeast metabolism. Using an overripe starter is possible, but you might want/need to reduce the starter-to-flour and water ratio in the leaven to dilute the acids. From time to time you should transfer your starter to a newly sterilised container.

If you only bake once or twice a week, keep your starter in the fridge, which will slow down its metabolism and reduce the frequency at which you need to refresh it, reducing your work and waste. You just need to remember to take it out, refresh it and leave at room/ambient temperature about a day before you need to make your leaven/production starter. See also the notes below on the effects of temperature on the cultures in your starter.

Longer-term storage

It is possible to both freeze and dry sourdough starter culture, though both will kill a number of the cells, so it will take a bit more time and effort in refreshment to revive your culture. To dry it, spread it thinly on a non-stick baking tray and put in a cool (less than 60°C) oven after baking. Once dry, the flakes of starter should be stored in a dry and airtight container in a cool, dark place.

Too much sourdough starter

A build-up of unused sourdough starter sometimes happens if your rate and amount of refreshment exceeds your use of it. This can be used at ratios of 5% or less to enhance almost any dough, apart from those where even a hint of acidity or discolouration would be unacceptable. Just add the old sourdough starter at dough mixing time along with the other ingredients. Other options are to pass it on to other would-be sourdough bakers, or use it to make sourdough crumpets, pancakes etc.

Controlling sourness

Sourdough doesn't have to be sour! While a slight tang might be to your (and your customers') taste, few people, if anyone, want sourdough to be mouth-puckering. If you are making sweet, enriched breads, you might prefer not to be able to detect any acidity at all

Lactobacilli (lactic acid bacteria) produce both lactic and acetic/ethanoic acids. A key part of mastering sourdough bread making is controlling the concentration and ratio of these acids. Too much acetic acid and the bread will taste very sour – it's the acid found in vinegar. If lactic acid dominates, the bread might have little in the way of discernible characteristics that some customers might have come expect, though others might prefer such a 'mild' version.

Different yeasts and bacteria are adapted to thrive in different conditions. Lactobacilli that produce higher levels of lactic acid tend to prefer wetter conditions at around 1-5°C, while those producing both lactic and acetic acid thrive better in lower hydration (stiffer) starters at around 20°C. Acetic acid is produced in lower quantities than lactic and so takes longer to build up in a dough.

To achieve a more pronounced flavour and sourness, try keeping your starter at a lower hydration (ie dough-like, with a higher flour to water ratio), keep it in the fridge between bakes and retard the dough you make using it. For a milder flavour and acidity, try nurturing a liquid starter, keep it at room temperature, refresh it more frequently and opt for ambient (rather than retarded) proving.

If wanting to make sourdough-leavened sweetened breads, consider using a pasta madre. This is a very stiff starter, kept under carefully controlled conditions, sometimes used by bakers for making bread such as panettone. Temperatures of between 25-30°C help to keep the production of acetic acid down, while putting the pasta madre in a bagnetto of sugar solution before a refreshment will help to draw the acid out.

Recipes

We've done the recipe book thing in *Slow Dough: Real Bread,* and there are many other repositories out there already, but here are just a few basic formulae.

Wholemeal bread

By Andrew Whitley. Made using baker's yeast in a straight process and ambient proving.

Ingredient	Baker's %	Weight
100% Wholemeal flour	100	516
Water	70	361
Fresh yeast	1.6	8
Salt	1.2	6
Olive oil or butter	3	15
Old dough*	18	93
Total	**193.8%**	**1000g**

*See pre-ferments on page 220.

Wholemeal flours of any type will need to have a higher hydration as the bran soaks up a lot of water. Mix and work to form a smooth and slightly elastic dough. Leave to bulk ferment for at least two hours, (preferably 3-4 hours) at 25°C. To develop some more strength during this time, fold the dough over on itself a few times. Scale and shape as desired. Bake at 230°C, turning the oven down to 200°C after the first 10 minutes. The remaining baking time will be about 30 minutes for large loaves, less for smaller ones.

Wholemeal bread

By Paul Barker of Cinnamon Square. Made using the sponge and dough method and ambient proving.

Sponge

Ingredient	Baker's %	Weight
Wholemeal bread flour	100	635
Water	50	317
Fresh yeast	1	6
Salt	1.5	10
Sourdough starter*	5	32
Total	**157.5%**	**1000g**

*Optional, to add flavour. Cinnamon Square's starter (the CS Sour) is made from rye flour and kept at 50-60% hydration.

This is a fairly stiff sponge. If using a mixer, five minutes on a slow speed should be enough to bring the ingredients together into a smooth dough. Remove from the mixer and leave for 18-24 hours in a covered container in a cool (15-20°C) room.

Ingredient	Baker's %	Weight
Wholemeal bread flour	100	479
Wholemeal sponge (above)	40	192
Water	65	311
Yeast	2	10
Salt	1.8	9
Total	**208.8%**	**1000g**

Mix all of the ingredients together to form a smooth dough. If using a mixer, this should take around three minutes on slow speed, followed by five minutes on fast. Bulk ferment for 3-5 hours. Scale and shape as desired, prove again until fully risen and bake at 230-240°C for 35-45 minutes for large loaves.

Everyday white bread

By Morgan Williams. Made using baker's yeast in a straight process and ambient proving.

Ingredient	Baker's %	Weight
White strong/bread flour	100	569
Water	60	341
Yeast	0.35	2
Salt	1.3	7.4
Total	**161.65%**	**1000g**

If you have a mixer, around three minutes at slow speed should be enough to combine the ingredients, followed by around five minutes on a faster speed to develop the gluten. The bulk proof will take around three to four hours, depending on the temperature of the water, flour and the bakery. During this time, you can fold the dough a couple of times if it needs some strength developing. After dividing/scaling and shaping, the final proof should take between an hour and a half and two hours. Bake at 230-240°C for 35-45 minutes.

Focaccia

By Morgan Williams.

Ingredient	Baker's %	Weight
White bread flour	100	520.8
Water (first hydration)	70	364.5
Water (second hydration)	10	52
Fresh yeast	2	10.5
Olive oil	8	41.8
Salt	2	10.5
Total	**192%**	**1000.1g**

This is a useful addition to your baking arsenal. You can scale individually or bake in a tray and then cut into pieces. You can rotate seasonal toppings to keep it interesting, use the dough to make ciabatta, and even use what you make as the basis of sandwiches.

As this is a very wet dough, you really need a mixer and it helps to hydrate it in two stages. Mix together the flour and most of the water for around five minutes on a slow speed. Leave to autolyse (see page 217) for at least 20 minutes. Add the yeast, salt and remaining water and mix for three minutes on slow speed. Switch to a fast speed and mix for a further 5-8 minutes, gradually adding the olive oil as you do. You should end up with very smooth, stretchy dough. Bulk prove at ambient temperature for around 3-4 hours, folding it a few times during this time.

Scale and shape as desired onto a well-oiled tray (4kg is good for a standard 18" x 30" tray) stretching as much as you can into the corners, trying not to tear the dough. Leave to rest for half an hour and stretch again to fill the tray. Leave to prove for another hour or so. Smooth a generous amount of olive oil over the dough and dimple well with your fingertips, right down to the tray. Optional toppings include rosemary and coarse salt.

Bake at about 210-220°C for around 20 minutes.

Fruit and nut bread

By Andrew Whitley. A sweet, enriched dough made using a sponge and dough method.

This can be used to make a fruited loaf or buns. It is easily adapted by omitting the fruit and nuts, or by adding one or more ground 'sweet' spices, such as cinnamon, clove, cardamom and allspice.

Sponge

Ingredient	Baker's %	Weight
Strong bread flour (white, wholemeal or a mixture)	100	130.1
Water (at 30°C)	73	95
Fresh yeast	3	3.9
Total	**176%**	**229g**

Mix, cover and ferment at ambient temperature for 12 to 20 hours.

Final dough

Ingredient	Baker's %	Weight
Strong bread flour (white, wholemeal or a mixture)	100	170.2
Overnight sponge	132	224.7
Butter	44	74.9
Egg	44	74.9
Sugar (preferably raw cane)	32	54.5
Chopped nuts and mixed dried fruit*	235	400.1
Salt	1	1.7
Total	**588%**	**1001g**

*The mixed fruits and nuts are best soaked overnight in water, fruit juice or an alcoholic drink, like rum or brandy. Any liquid that has not been absorbed overnight may be used to replace an equal amount of the water when making the final dough.

Mix everything except the fruit and nut mix to form a soft dough. Fold in the fruits and nuts until evenly distributed, taking care not to over mix, which will pulp the fruit. Bulk prove for two hours. Divide, shape and prove again. Bake in a moderate (approximately 180°C) oven to prevent burning. Small loaves will take around 30-40 minutes.

Laminated dough

By Andrew Whitley.

This can be used for viennoiserie (eg croissants, pains au chocolat) and other light, flaky products.

Ingredient	Baker's %	Weight
Strong white flour	100	600
Scalded milk	62.5	375
Fresh yeast	2.91	17.5
Salt	1.25	7.5
Total	**166.66%**	**1000g**

Plus: 250g/41.67% butter (refrigerated) to laminate.

Mix the first four ingredients together and work to form dough of fairly firm consistency. Chill to 10°C.

Roll the dough out to a rectangle about 10mm thick. Roll out the butter to cover two-thirds of the dough. Fold in three, roll out and fold in three again (ie a half turn). Return to the fridge/chiller for minimum 30-90 minutes.

Roll the chilled dough out a little longer than before and give a 'book turn', ie fold the side edges to the middle and then fold in half along this centre line. Return to the fridge/chiller for 30-90 minutes. Following this pattern of turns should produce 24 layers of butter between the layers of dough.

Finally roll out to about 4mm thick and cut out right-angled triangles for croissants or rectangles for pains au chocolat. Roll up, glaze with egg, prove for about 30-60 minutes and bake at 200°C for 15 minutes.

White sourdough bread

By Andrew Whitley.

Leaven

Ingredient	Baker's %	Weight
White bread flour	75	150
Wholemeal bread flour	25	50
Warm water	60	120
Liquid (100% hydration) sourdough starter	80	160
Total	**240%**	**480g**

Mix together and ferment for around four hours at ambient (20-25°C) or for about 12 hours at 8-12°C.

Final dough

Ingredient	Baker's %	Weight
White bread flour	75	300
Wholemeal bread flour	25	100
Warm water	75	300
Leaven (from above)	75	300
Salt	2	8
Total	**252%**	**1008g**

Mix the ingredients together to form a smooth dough, preferably adding the leaven towards the end of mixing. Bulk prove for 3-4 hours at ambient temperature. Scale and shape as desired and place in proving dusted baskets or couches. Prove again for 1-2 hours and bake at 230°C for around 35-45 minutes for large loaves.

100% rye sourdough bread

By Andrew Whitley.

Rye starter

Day 1

Ingredient	Bakers %	Weight
Wholemeal rye flour	100	25
Warm water (30°C)	200	50
Total	**300%**	**75g**

Mix, cover and ferment at as close to 30°C as possible for 24 hours.

Day 2

Ingredient	Bakers %	Weight
Wholemeal rye flour	100	25
Warm water (30°C)	200	50
Starter from day 1	300	75
Total	**600%**	**150g**

Method as above.

Day 3

Ingredient	Bakers %	Weight
Wholemeal rye flour	100	25
Warm Water (30°C)	200	50
Starter from day 2	600	150
Total	**900%**	**225g**

Method as above.

Day 4

Ingredient	Bakers %	Weight
Wholemeal rye flour	100	30
Warm water (30°C)	150	45
Starter from day 3	750	225
Total	**1000%**	**300g**

Method as above. You should now have a vigorous starter. If not, repeat the last step for another day or two until it is. You can then use this sourdough starter to make a leaven, as in the following recipe, retaining and refreshing the remainder for future baking.

Leaven

Ingredient	Bakers %	Weight
Wholemeal rye flour	100	150
Warm water (30°C)	200	300
Rye starter (from above)	33.3	50
Total	**333.3%**	**500g**

Mix together, cover and ferment for 12-24 hours at warm ambient temperature (25-30°C).

Final dough

Ingredient	Bakers %	Weight
Rye flour (wholemeal or light)	100	340
Water	61.76	210
Leaven (from above)	132.35	450
Salt	1.47	5
Total	**295.58%**	**1005g**

Mix together to form a very sloppy dough. Scale (approximately 930g for an 800g loaf and 480g for a 400g one) and scoop the dough into greased tins to prove. If the tin was half full when you started, then the dough will be ready when it has almost reached the top. Proving could take anything from two to eight hours, depending on the vigour of your starter and the ambient temperature – this is something that you will just have to learn from the experience of baking with your own starter in your own bakehouse.

Bake at 240°C for 10 minutes and then reduce to 220°C. Continue baking for a further 40-50 minutes (large loaves) or 25-35 minutes (small loaves).

As rye bread like this is very sticky and difficult to slice immediately after baking, it can (and perhaps should) be sold the day after baking. The natural preservative and anti-staling effect of the lactic acid bacteria in the starter means that the loaf will remain good to eat for perhaps a week.

Roll of honour

Our backers

The original edition of this book was funded by Sustain, The Big Lottery's Local Food Fund and The Sheepdrove Trust.

The first run of the 2021 edition was crowdfunded by more than 270 lovely doughnors. They included:

Bread Source   Two Magpies Bakery   The Welbeck Bakehouse

and

Chris Brennan, Keisha Burch, Francis Cooper, Kath Dalmeny, Gerry Danby, Hugh Fearnley-Whittingstall, Matt Fountain, Nettie Francis, Anthony Golledge, Trevor Gulliver, Katia Lebart (Wee Boulangerie), Stephanie Mathern, Douglas Muir, Andrew Neagle (Anuna Craft Bakehouse), Dara O'hArtghaile, Redbournbury Watermill, Ben Reynolds, Gareth Roberts, Steven Rule, Eddy Sleiman, T. Wade.

and

Toby Anstruther, Tom Baker, Stephen Barkley, Steve Bath, Jim Bennett, Paul Billyard, Paul Brennan, Chris Brownlow, Graham Capper, Helen Constantinou, Mary Cooper, Sam Cornish, Kath Dalmeny, James Doig, Catherine Drennan, Colin Fallon, Megan Fitzoliver, Flour and Spoon Bakery, Duncan Glendinning, Tara Heron, Jo's Loaves, John King, Christine Lindop, Loaf Affair, Loaf Bakery, Angela Lomax, Tim Marsden, Mission Pizza, Aidan Monks, A and P Morgan, Keith Moscrop, Charlotte Nemeth, Orkney Sourdough, Dr. Ian Parker, Emma Parkin, Cristina Schwarz, Susan Shaw, Robin Van Creveld, Colin Welch, Stephanie Young.

Thanks to you all, and the rest of our supporters, for the dough to do it!

Credits

Knead to Know...more
Chris Young and bakers of the Real Bread Campaign
ISBN 978-1-903060-67-4

This edition first published in 2021 by
Sustain: the alliance for better food and farming.
244-254 Cambridge Heath Road, London E2 9DA
realbread@sustainweb.org
www.sustainweb.org
www.therealbreadcampaign.org

Design and layout by Alan Karlik.
Typeset in Sentient and Apfel Grotezk. Printed in England by RAP Spiderweb.

This book was a team effort and Chris thanks everyone who volunteered their time and utterly indispensable knowledge, advice, opinion, design, proofreading and other assistance with one or both editions. They include: Romilla Arber, Tom Baker, Paul Barker, Jade Bashford, Troels Bendix, Richard Bertinet, Maressa Bossano, Keith Bohanna, Johanna Bottrill, George Casey, Corinne Castle, Aidan Chapman, Feline Charpentier, Susan Clarke, Simon Cobb, Clive Cobb, Peter Cook, Anne Dolamore, Markus Drayss, Carmen Facio, Andrew Forbes, John Forrester, Dave Foster, Kirsten Foster, Debbie Galton, Mark Gatenby, Duncan Glendinning, Russell Goodwin, Emmanuel Hadjiandreou, Mike Hampson, Sophie Handschuh, Colin Hilder, Nick Jones, Sally Lane, John Letts, John Lister, Cath Lloyd-Williams, Dave Lomax, Anthony Long, Pilar Lopez, Ben Mackinnon, Clare Marriage, Jane Mason, Dan McTiernan, Paul Merry, Adam Pagor, Emma Parkin, Maggie Rich, Steve Rickaby, Lauren Ritchie, Natasha Soares, Mark Stambler, Lucie Steel, Alison Swan-Parente, Alex Tait, Devika Tamang, Sue Tennyson, Kathryn Warhurst, Ian Waterland, Richard Watts, Andrew Whitley, Louise Williams, Morgan Williams, Liz Wilson, Julie Zieberg, Cindy Zurias.

Chris also thanks his family for ongoing love and support; Kath Dalmeny, Gavin Dupée, Jeanette Longfield, Charlie Powell, Ben Reynolds, Quoc-anh Tran, Sarah Williams and the rest of the Sustain family present and past; all Campaign ambassadors, supporters and volunteers over the years; and you for buying this book. He's sorry to anyone missed off the list. This one's for Arttu.

Photos on these pages were taken at:

34	Alex Gooch market stall, September 2009
42	Clervaux Artisan Bakery, February 2013
54	Real Bread Festival, October 2012
60	A market in Lille, November 2010
70	Denver Mill, November 2010
74	Simit stall in Istanbul, April 2012
100	The Old Post Office Bakery, October 2019
124	Aries Bakehouse, March 2021
144	E5 Bakehouse, September 2019
166	Brook Food Processing Equipment, July 2018
174	Shipton Mill test bakery, December 2010
184	Real Bread Festival, October 2012
216	Denver Mill, November 2010
230	Better Health Bakery, September 2019